C-1073 CAREER EXAMINATION SERIES

This is your
PASSBOOK for...

Accounting Analyst

Test Preparation Study Guide
Questions & Answers

COPYRIGHT NOTICE

This book is SOLELY intended for, is sold ONLY to, and its use is RESTRICTED to individual, bona fide applicants or candidates who qualify by virtue of having seriously filed applications for appropriate license, certificate, professional and/or promotional advancement, higher school matriculation, scholarship, or other legitimate requirements of education and/or governmental authorities.

This book is NOT intended for use, class instruction, tutoring, training, duplication, copying, reprinting, excerption, or adaptation, etc., by:

1) Other publishers
2) Proprietors and/or Instructors of "Coaching" and/or Preparatory Courses
3) Personnel and/or Training Divisions of commercial, industrial, and governmental organizations
4) Schools, colleges, or universities and/or their departments and staffs, including teachers and other personnel
5) Testing Agencies or Bureaus
6) Study groups which seek by the purchase of a single volume to copy and/or duplicate and/or adapt this material for use by the group as a whole without having purchased individual volumes for each of the members of the group
7) Et al.

Such persons would be in violation of appropriate Federal and State statutes.

PROVISION OF LICENSING AGREEMENTS – Recognized educational, commercial, industrial, and governmental institutions and organizations, and others legitimately engaged in educational pursuits, including training, testing, and measurement activities, may address request for a licensing agreement to the copyright owners, who will determine whether, and under what conditions, including fees and charges, the materials in this book may be used them. In other words, a licensing facility exists for the legitimate use of the material in this book on other than an individual basis. However, it is asseverated and affirmed here that the material in this book CANNOT be used without the receipt of the express permission of such a licensing agreement from the Publishers. Inquiries re licensing should be addressed to the company, attention rights and permissions department.

All rights reserved, including the right of reproduction in whole or in part, in any form or by any means, electronic or mechanical, including photocopying, recording, or by any information storage and retrieval system, without permission in writing from the Publisher.

Copyright © 2024 by
National Learning Corporation

212 Michael Drive, Syosset, NY 11791
(516) 921-8888 • www.passbooks.com
E-mail: info@passbooks.com

PUBLISHED IN THE UNITED STATES OF AMERICA

PASSBOOK® SERIES

THE *PASSBOOK® SERIES* has been created to prepare applicants and candidates for the ultimate academic battlefield – the examination room.

At some time in our lives, each and every one of us may be required to take an examination – for validation, matriculation, admission, qualification, registration, certification, or licensure.

Based on the assumption that every applicant or candidate has met the basic formal educational standards, has taken the required number of courses, and read the necessary texts, the *PASSBOOK® SERIES* furnishes the one special preparation which may assure passing with confidence, instead of failing with insecurity. Examination questions – together with answers – are furnished as the basic vehicle for study so that the mysteries of the examination and its compounding difficulties may be eliminated or diminished by a sure method.

This book is meant to help you pass your examination provided that you qualify and are serious in your objective.

The entire field is reviewed through the huge store of content information which is succinctly presented through a provocative and challenging approach – the question-and-answer method.

A climate of success is established by furnishing the correct answers at the end of each test.

You soon learn to recognize types of questions, forms of questions, and patterns of questioning. You may even begin to anticipate expected outcomes.

You perceive that many questions are repeated or adapted so that you can gain acute insights, which may enable you to score many sure points.

You learn how to confront new questions, or types of questions, and to attack them confidently and work out the correct answers.

You note objectives and emphases, and recognize pitfalls and dangers, so that you may make positive educational adjustments.

Moreover, you are kept fully informed in relation to new concepts, methods, practices, and directions in the field.

You discover that you are actually taking the examination all the time: you are preparing for the examination by "taking" an examination, not by reading extraneous and/or supererogatory textbooks.

In short, this PASSBOOK®, used directedly, should be an important factor in helping you to pass your test.

ACCOUNTING ANALYST

This is the recruiting, developmental and first journey level class in this series, for persons qualified to perform analytical, forecasting, planning and/or advisory duties in the area of accounting.

SCOPE OF THE EXAMINATION
The written test will cover knowledge, skills, and/or abilities in such areas as:
1. Principles of accounting;
2. Governmental accounting;
3. Analyzing and interpreting data;
4. Written communication; and
5. Workplace scenarios.

HOW TO TAKE A TEST

I. YOU MUST PASS AN EXAMINATION

A. WHAT EVERY CANDIDATE SHOULD KNOW

Examination applicants often ask us for help in preparing for the written test. What can I study in advance? What kinds of questions will be asked? How will the test be given? How will the papers be graded?

As an applicant for a civil service examination, you may be wondering about some of these things. Our purpose here is to suggest effective methods of advance study and to describe civil service examinations.

Your chances for success on this examination can be increased if you know how to prepare. Those "pre-examination jitters" can be reduced if you know what to expect. You can even experience an adventure in good citizenship if you know why civil service exams are given.

B. WHY ARE CIVIL SERVICE EXAMINATIONS GIVEN?

Civil service examinations are important to you in two ways. As a citizen, you want public jobs filled by employees who know how to do their work. As a job seeker, you want a fair chance to compete for that job on an equal footing with other candidates. The best-known means of accomplishing this two-fold goal is the competitive examination.

Exams are widely publicized throughout the nation. They may be administered for jobs in federal, state, city, municipal, town or village governments or agencies.

Any citizen may apply, with some limitations, such as the age or residence of applicants. Your experience and education may be reviewed to see whether you meet the requirements for the particular examination. When these requirements exist, they are reasonable and applied consistently to all applicants. Thus, a competitive examination may cause you some uneasiness now, but it is your privilege and safeguard.

C. HOW ARE CIVIL SERVICE EXAMS DEVELOPED?

Examinations are carefully written by trained technicians who are specialists in the field known as "psychological measurement," in consultation with recognized authorities in the field of work that the test will cover. These experts recommend the subject matter areas or skills to be tested; only those knowledges or skills important to your success on the job are included. The most reliable books and source materials available are used as references. Together, the experts and technicians judge the difficulty level of the questions.

Test technicians know how to phrase questions so that the problem is clearly stated. Their ethics do not permit "trick" or "catch" questions. Questions may have been tried out on sample groups, or subjected to statistical analysis, to determine their usefulness.

Written tests are often used in combination with performance tests, ratings of training and experience, and oral interviews. All of these measures combine to form the best-known means of finding the right person for the right job.

II. HOW TO PASS THE WRITTEN TEST

A. NATURE OF THE EXAMINATION

To prepare intelligently for civil service examinations, you should know how they differ from school examinations you have taken. In school you were assigned certain definite pages to read or subjects to cover. The examination questions were quite detailed and usually emphasized memory. Civil service exams, on the other hand, try to discover your present ability to perform the duties of a position, plus your potentiality to learn these duties. In other words, a civil service exam attempts to predict how successful you will be. Questions cover such a broad area that they cannot be as minute and detailed as school exam questions.

In the public service similar kinds of work, or positions, are grouped together in one "class." This process is known as *position-classification*. All the positions in a class are paid according to the salary range for that class. One class title covers all of these positions, and they are all tested by the same examination.

B. FOUR BASIC STEPS

1) Study the announcement

How, then, can you know what subjects to study? Our best answer is: "Learn as much as possible about the class of positions for which you've applied." The exam will test the knowledge, skills and abilities needed to do the work.

Your most valuable source of information about the position you want is the official exam announcement. This announcement lists the training and experience qualifications. Check these standards and apply only if you come reasonably close to meeting them.

The brief description of the position in the examination announcement offers some clues to the subjects which will be tested. Think about the job itself. Review the duties in your mind. Can you perform them, or are there some in which you are rusty? Fill in the blank spots in your preparation.

Many jurisdictions preview the written test in the exam announcement by including a section called "Knowledge and Abilities Required," "Scope of the Examination," or some similar heading. Here you will find out specifically what fields will be tested.

2) Review your own background

Once you learn in general what the position is all about, and what you need to know to do the work, ask yourself which subjects you already know fairly well and which need improvement. You may wonder whether to concentrate on improving your strong areas or on building some background in your fields of weakness. When the announcement has specified "some knowledge" or "considerable knowledge," or has used adjectives like "beginning principles of..." or "advanced ... methods," you can get a clue as to the number and difficulty of questions to be asked in any given field. More questions, and hence broader coverage, would be included for those subjects which are more important in the work. Now weigh your strengths and weaknesses against the job requirements and prepare accordingly.

3) Determine the level of the position

Another way to tell how intensively you should prepare is to understand the level of the job for which you are applying. Is it the entering level? In other words, is this the position in which beginners in a field of work are hired? Or is it an intermediate or advanced level? Sometimes this is indicated by such words as "Junior" or "Senior" in the class title. Other jurisdictions use Roman numerals to designate the level – Clerk I, Clerk II, for example. The word "Supervisor" sometimes appears in the title. If the level is not indicated by the title, check the description of duties. Will you be working under very close supervision, or will you have responsibility for independent decisions in this work?

4) Choose appropriate study materials

Now that you know the subjects to be examined and the relative amount of each subject to be covered, you can choose suitable study materials. For beginning level jobs, or even advanced ones, if you have a pronounced weakness in some aspect of your training, read a modern, standard textbook in that field. Be sure it is up to date and has general coverage. Such books are normally available at your library, and the librarian will be glad to help you locate one. For entry-level positions, questions of appropriate difficulty are chosen – neither highly advanced questions, nor those too simple. Such questions require careful thought but not advanced training.

If the position for which you are applying is technical or advanced, you will read more advanced, specialized material. If you are already familiar with the basic principles of your field, elementary textbooks would waste your time. Concentrate on advanced textbooks and technical periodicals. Think through the concepts and review difficult problems in your field.

These are all general sources. You can get more ideas on your own initiative, following these leads. For example, training manuals and publications of the government agency which employs workers in your field can be useful, particularly for technical and professional positions. A letter or visit to the government department involved may result in more specific study suggestions, and certainly will provide you with a more definite idea of the exact nature of the position you are seeking.

III. KINDS OF TESTS

Tests are used for purposes other than measuring knowledge and ability to perform specified duties. For some positions, it is equally important to test ability to make adjustments to new situations or to profit from training. In others, basic mental abilities not dependent on information are essential. Questions which test these things may not appear as pertinent to the duties of the position as those which test for knowledge and information. Yet they are often highly important parts of a fair examination. For very general questions, it is almost impossible to help you direct your study efforts. What we can do is to point out some of the more common of these general abilities needed in public service positions and describe some typical questions.

1) General information

Broad, general information has been found useful for predicting job success in some kinds of work. This is tested in a variety of ways, from vocabulary lists to questions about current events. Basic background in some field of work, such as sociology or economics, may be sampled in a group of questions. Often these are principles which have become familiar to most persons through exposure rather than through formal training. It is difficult to advise you how to study for these questions; being alert to the world around you is our best suggestion.

2) Verbal ability

An example of an ability needed in many positions is verbal or language ability. Verbal ability is, in brief, the ability to use and understand words. Vocabulary and grammar tests are typical measures of this ability. Reading comprehension or paragraph interpretation questions are common in many kinds of civil service tests. You are given a paragraph of written material and asked to find its central meaning.

3) Numerical ability

Number skills can be tested by the familiar arithmetic problem, by checking paired lists of numbers to see which are alike and which are different, or by interpreting charts and graphs. In the latter test, a graph may be printed in the test booklet which you are asked to use as the basis for answering questions.

4) Observation

A popular test for law-enforcement positions is the observation test. A picture is shown to you for several minutes, then taken away. Questions about the picture test your ability to observe both details and larger elements.

5) Following directions

In many positions in the public service, the employee must be able to carry out written instructions dependably and accurately. You may be given a chart with several columns, each column listing a variety of information. The questions require you to carry out directions involving the information given in the chart.

6) Skills and aptitudes

Performance tests effectively measure some manual skills and aptitudes. When the skill is one in which you are trained, such as typing or shorthand, you can practice. These tests are often very much like those given in business school or high school courses. For many of the other skills and aptitudes, however, no short-time preparation can be made. Skills and abilities natural to you or that you have developed throughout your lifetime are being tested.

Many of the general questions just described provide all the data needed to answer the questions and ask you to use your reasoning ability to find the answers. Your best preparation for these tests, as well as for tests of facts and ideas, is to be at your physical and mental best. You, no doubt, have your own methods of getting into an exam-taking mood and keeping "in shape." The next section lists some ideas on this subject.

IV. KINDS OF QUESTIONS

Only rarely is the "essay" question, which you answer in narrative form, used in civil service tests. Civil service tests are usually of the short-answer type. Full instructions for answering these questions will be given to you at the examination. But in case this is your first experience with short-answer questions and separate answer sheets, here is what you need to know:

1) **Multiple-choice Questions**

Most popular of the short-answer questions is the "multiple choice" or "best answer" question. It can be used, for example, to test for factual knowledge, ability to solve problems or judgment in meeting situations found at work.

A multiple-choice question is normally one of three types—
- It can begin with an incomplete statement followed by several possible endings. You are to find the one ending which *best* completes the statement, although some of the others may not be entirely wrong.
- It can also be a complete statement in the form of a question which is answered by choosing one of the statements listed.

- It can be in the form of a problem – again you select the best answer.

Here is an example of a multiple-choice question with a discussion which should give you some clues as to the method for choosing the right answer:

When an employee has a complaint about his assignment, the action which will *best* help him overcome his difficulty is to
- A. discuss his difficulty with his coworkers
- B. take the problem to the head of the organization
- C. take the problem to the person who gave him the assignment
- D. say nothing to anyone about his complaint

In answering this question, you should study each of the choices to find which is best. Consider choice "A" – Certainly an employee may discuss his complaint with fellow employees, but no change or improvement can result, and the complaint remains unresolved. Choice "B" is a poor choice since the head of the organization probably does not know what assignment you have been given, and taking your problem to him is known as "going over the head" of the supervisor. The supervisor, or person who made the assignment, is the person who can clarify it or correct any injustice. Choice "C" is, therefore, correct. To say nothing, as in choice "D," is unwise. Supervisors have and interest in knowing the problems employees are facing, and the employee is seeking a solution to his problem.

2) True/False Questions

The "true/false" or "right/wrong" form of question is sometimes used. Here a complete statement is given. Your job is to decide whether the statement is right or wrong.

SAMPLE: A roaming cell-phone call to a nearby city costs less than a non-roaming call to a distant city.

This statement is wrong, or false, since roaming calls are more expensive.

This is not a complete list of all possible question forms, although most of the others are variations of these common types. You will always get complete directions for answering questions. Be sure you understand *how* to mark your answers – ask questions until you do.

V. RECORDING YOUR ANSWERS

Computer terminals are used more and more today for many different kinds of exams.

For an examination with very few applicants, you may be told to record your answers in the test booklet itself. Separate answer sheets are much more common. If this separate answer sheet is to be scored by machine – and this is often the case – it is highly important that you mark your answers correctly in order to get credit.

An electronic scoring machine is often used in civil service offices because of the speed with which papers can be scored. Machine-scored answer sheets must be marked with a pencil, which will be given to you. This pencil has a high graphite content which responds to the electronic scoring machine. As a matter of fact, stray dots may register as answers, so do not let your pencil rest on the answer sheet while you are pondering the correct answer. Also, if your pencil lead breaks or is otherwise defective, ask for another.

Since the answer sheet will be dropped in a slot in the scoring machine, be careful not to bend the corners or get the paper crumpled.

The answer sheet normally has five vertical columns of numbers, with 30 numbers to a column. These numbers correspond to the question numbers in your test booklet. After each number, going across the page are four or five pairs of dotted lines. These short dotted lines have small letters or numbers above them. The first two pairs may also have a "T" or "F" above the letters. This indicates that the first two pairs only are to be used if the questions are of the true-false type. If the questions are multiple choice, disregard the "T" and "F" and pay attention only to the small letters or numbers.

Answer your questions in the manner of the sample that follows:

32. The largest city in the United States is
    A. Washington, D.C.
    B. New York City
    C. Chicago
    D. Detroit
    E. San Francisco

1) Choose the answer you think is best. (New York City is the largest, so "B" is correct.)
2) Find the row of dotted lines numbered the same as the question you are answering. (Find row number 32)
3) Find the pair of dotted lines corresponding to the answer. (Find the pair of lines under the mark "B.")
4) Make a solid black mark between the dotted lines.

VI. BEFORE THE TEST

Common sense will help you find procedures to follow to get ready for an examination. Too many of us, however, overlook these sensible measures. Indeed, nervousness and fatigue have been found to be the most serious reasons why applicants fail to do their best on civil service tests. Here is a list of reminders:

- Begin your preparation early – Don't wait until the last minute to go scurrying around for books and materials or to find out what the position is all about.
- Prepare continuously – An hour a night for a week is better than an all-night cram session. This has been definitely established. What is more, a night a week for a month will return better dividends than crowding your study into a shorter period of time.
- Locate the place of the exam – You have been sent a notice telling you when and where to report for the examination. If the location is in a different town or otherwise unfamiliar to you, it would be well to inquire the best route and learn something about the building.
- Relax the night before the test – Allow your mind to rest. Do not study at all that night. Plan some mild recreation or diversion; then go to bed early and get a good night's sleep.
- Get up early enough to make a leisurely trip to the place for the test – This way unforeseen events, traffic snarls, unfamiliar buildings, etc. will not upset you.
- Dress comfortably – A written test is not a fashion show. You will be known by number and not by name, so wear something comfortable.

- Leave excess paraphernalia at home – Shopping bags and odd bundles will get in your way. You need bring only the items mentioned in the official notice you received; usually everything you need is provided. Do not bring reference books to the exam. They will only confuse those last minutes and be taken away from you when in the test room.
- Arrive somewhat ahead of time – If because of transportation schedules you must get there very early, bring a newspaper or magazine to take your mind off yourself while waiting.
- Locate the examination room – When you have found the proper room, you will be directed to the seat or part of the room where you will sit. Sometimes you are given a sheet of instructions to read while you are waiting. Do not fill out any forms until you are told to do so; just read them and be prepared.
- Relax and prepare to listen to the instructions
- If you have any physical problem that may keep you from doing your best, be sure to tell the test administrator. If you are sick or in poor health, you really cannot do your best on the exam. You can come back and take the test some other time.

VII. AT THE TEST

The day of the test is here and you have the test booklet in your hand. The temptation to get going is very strong. Caution! There is more to success than knowing the right answers. You must know how to identify your papers and understand variations in the type of short-answer question used in this particular examination. Follow these suggestions for maximum results from your efforts:

1) Cooperate with the monitor

The test administrator has a duty to create a situation in which you can be as much at ease as possible. He will give instructions, tell you when to begin, check to see that you are marking your answer sheet correctly, and so on. He is not there to guard you, although he will see that your competitors do not take unfair advantage. He wants to help you do your best.

2) Listen to all instructions

Don't jump the gun! Wait until you understand all directions. In most civil service tests you get more time than you need to answer the questions. So don't be in a hurry. Read each word of instructions until you clearly understand the meaning. Study the examples, listen to all announcements and follow directions. Ask questions if you do not understand what to do.

3) Identify your papers

Civil service exams are usually identified by number only. You will be assigned a number; you must not put your name on your test papers. Be sure to copy your number correctly. Since more than one exam may be given, copy your exact examination title.

4) Plan your time

Unless you are told that a test is a "speed" or "rate of work" test, speed itself is usually not important. Time enough to answer all the questions will be provided, but this does not mean that you have all day. An overall time limit has been set. Divide the total time (in minutes) by the number of questions to determine the approximate time you have for each question.

5) Do not linger over difficult questions

If you come across a difficult question, mark it with a paper clip (useful to have along) and come back to it when you have been through the booklet. One caution if you do this – be sure to skip a number on your answer sheet as well. Check often to be sure that you have not lost your place and that you are marking in the row numbered the same as the question you are answering.

6) Read the questions

Be sure you know what the question asks! Many capable people are unsuccessful because they failed to *read* the questions correctly.

7) Answer all questions

Unless you have been instructed that a penalty will be deducted for incorrect answers, it is better to guess than to omit a question.

8) Speed tests

It is often better NOT to guess on speed tests. It has been found that on timed tests people are tempted to spend the last few seconds before time is called in marking answers at random – without even reading them – in the hope of picking up a few extra points. To discourage this practice, the instructions may warn you that your score will be "corrected" for guessing. That is, a penalty will be applied. The incorrect answers will be deducted from the correct ones, or some other penalty formula will be used.

9) Review your answers

If you finish before time is called, go back to the questions you guessed or omitted to give them further thought. Review other answers if you have time.

10) Return your test materials

If you are ready to leave before others have finished or time is called, take ALL your materials to the monitor and leave quietly. Never take any test material with you. The monitor can discover whose papers are not complete, and taking a test booklet may be grounds for disqualification.

VIII. EXAMINATION TECHNIQUES

1) Read the general instructions carefully. These are usually printed on the first page of the exam booklet. As a rule, these instructions refer to the timing of the examination; the fact that you should not start work until the signal and must stop work at a signal, etc. If there are any *special* instructions, such as a choice of questions to be answered, make sure that you note this instruction carefully.

2) When you are ready to start work on the examination, that is as soon as the signal has been given, read the instructions to each question booklet, underline any key words or phrases, such as *least, best, outline, describe* and the like. In this way you will tend to answer as requested rather than discover on reviewing your paper that you *listed without describing*, that you selected the *worst* choice rather than the *best* choice, etc.

3) If the examination is of the objective or multiple-choice type – that is, each question will also give a series of possible answers: A, B, C or D, and you are called upon to select the best answer and write the letter next to that answer on your answer paper – it is advisable to start answering each question in turn. There may be anywhere from 50 to 100 such questions in the three or four hours allotted and you can see how much time would be taken if you read through all the questions before beginning to answer any. Furthermore, if you come across a question or group of questions which you know would be difficult to answer, it would undoubtedly affect your handling of all the other questions.

4) If the examination is of the essay type and contains but a few questions, it is a moot point as to whether you should read all the questions before starting to answer any one. Of course, if you are given a choice – say five out of seven and the like – then it is essential to read all the questions so you can eliminate the two that are most difficult. If, however, you are asked to answer all the questions, there may be danger in trying to answer the easiest one first because you may find that you will spend too much time on it. The best technique is to answer the first question, then proceed to the second, etc.

5) Time your answers. Before the exam begins, write down the time it started, then add the time allowed for the examination and write down the time it must be completed, then divide the time available somewhat as follows:
   - If 3-1/2 hours are allowed, that would be 210 minutes. If you have 80 objective-type questions, that would be an average of 2-1/2 minutes per question. Allow yourself no more than 2 minutes per question, or a total of 160 minutes, which will permit about 50 minutes to review.
   - If for the time allotment of 210 minutes there are 7 essay questions to answer, that would average about 30 minutes a question. Give yourself only 25 minutes per question so that you have about 35 minutes to review.

6) The most important instruction is to *read each question* and make sure you know what is wanted. The second most important instruction is to *time yourself properly* so that you answer every question. The third most important instruction is to *answer every question*. Guess if you have to but include something for each question. Remember that you will receive no credit for a blank and will probably receive some credit if you write something in answer to an essay question. If you guess a letter – say "B" for a multiple-choice question – you may have guessed right. If you leave a blank as an answer to a multiple-choice question, the examiners may respect your feelings but it will not add a point to your score. Some exams may penalize you for wrong answers, so in such cases *only*, you may not want to guess unless you have some basis for your answer.

7) Suggestions
   a. Objective-type questions
      1. Examine the question booklet for proper sequence of pages and questions
      2. Read all instructions carefully
      3. Skip any question which seems too difficult; return to it after all other questions have been answered
      4. Apportion your time properly; do not spend too much time on any single question or group of questions

5. Note and underline key words – *all, most, fewest, least, best, worst, same, opposite,* etc.
6. Pay particular attention to negatives
7. Note unusual option, e.g., unduly long, short, complex, different or similar in content to the body of the question
8. Observe the use of "hedging" words – *probably, may, most likely,* etc.
9. Make sure that your answer is put next to the same number as the question
10. Do not second-guess unless you have good reason to believe the second answer is definitely more correct
11. Cross out original answer if you decide another answer is more accurate; do not erase until you are ready to hand your paper in
12. Answer all questions; guess unless instructed otherwise
13. Leave time for review

   b. Essay questions
     1. Read each question carefully
     2. Determine exactly what is wanted. Underline key words or phrases.
     3. Decide on outline or paragraph answer
     4. Include many different points and elements unless asked to develop any one or two points or elements
     5. Show impartiality by giving pros and cons unless directed to select one side only
     6. Make and write down any assumptions you find necessary to answer the questions
     7. Watch your English, grammar, punctuation and choice of words
     8. Time your answers; don't crowd material

8) Answering the essay question

Most essay questions can be answered by framing the specific response around several key words or ideas. Here are a few such key words or ideas:

M's: manpower, materials, methods, money, management
P's: purpose, program, policy, plan, procedure, practice, problems, pitfalls, personnel, public relations
   a. Six basic steps in handling problems:
     1. Preliminary plan and background development
     2. Collect information, data and facts
     3. Analyze and interpret information, data and facts
     4. Analyze and develop solutions as well as make recommendations
     5. Prepare report and sell recommendations
     6. Install recommendations and follow up effectiveness

   b. Pitfalls to avoid
     1. *Taking things for granted* – A statement of the situation does not necessarily imply that each of the elements is necessarily true; for example, a complaint may be invalid and biased so that all that can be taken for granted is that a complaint has been registered

2. *Considering only one side of a situation* – Wherever possible, indicate several alternatives and then point out the reasons you selected the best one
3. *Failing to indicate follow up* – Whenever your answer indicates action on your part, make certain that you will take proper follow-up action to see how successful your recommendations, procedures or actions turn out to be
4. *Taking too long in answering any single question* – Remember to time your answers properly

IX. AFTER THE TEST

Scoring procedures differ in detail among civil service jurisdictions although the general principles are the same. Whether the papers are hand-scored or graded by machine we have described, they are nearly always graded by number. That is, the person who marks the paper knows only the number – never the name – of the applicant. Not until all the papers have been graded will they be matched with names. If other tests, such as training and experience or oral interview ratings have been given, scores will be combined. Different parts of the examination usually have different weights. For example, the written test might count 60 percent of the final grade, and a rating of training and experience 40 percent. In many jurisdictions, veterans will have a certain number of points added to their grades.

After the final grade has been determined, the names are placed in grade order and an eligible list is established. There are various methods for resolving ties between those who get the same final grade – probably the most common is to place first the name of the person whose application was received first. Job offers are made from the eligible list in the order the names appear on it. You will be notified of your grade and your rank as soon as all these computations have been made. This will be done as rapidly as possible.

People who are found to meet the requirements in the announcement are called "eligibles." Their names are put on a list of eligible candidates. An eligible's chances of getting a job depend on how high he stands on this list and how fast agencies are filling jobs from the list.

When a job is to be filled from a list of eligibles, the agency asks for the names of people on the list of eligibles for that job. When the civil service commission receives this request, it sends to the agency the names of the three people highest on this list. Or, if the job to be filled has specialized requirements, the office sends the agency the names of the top three persons who meet these requirements from the general list.

The appointing officer makes a choice from among the three people whose names were sent to him. If the selected person accepts the appointment, the names of the others are put back on the list to be considered for future openings.

That is the rule in hiring from all kinds of eligible lists, whether they are for typist, carpenter, chemist, or something else. For every vacancy, the appointing officer has his choice of any one of the top three eligibles on the list. This explains why the person whose name is on top of the list sometimes does not get an appointment when some of the persons lower on the list do. If the appointing officer chooses the second or third eligible, the No. 1 eligible does not get a job at once, but stays on the list until he is appointed or the list is terminated.

X. HOW TO PASS THE INTERVIEW TEST

The examination for which you applied requires an oral interview test. You have already taken the written test and you are now being called for the interview test – the final part of the formal examination.

You may think that it is not possible to prepare for an interview test and that there are no procedures to follow during an interview. Our purpose is to point out some things you can do in advance that will help you and some good rules to follow and pitfalls to avoid while you are being interviewed.

What is an interview supposed to test?

The written examination is designed to test the technical knowledge and competence of the candidate; the oral is designed to evaluate intangible qualities, not readily measured otherwise, and to establish a list showing the relative fitness of each candidate – as measured against his competitors – for the position sought. Scoring is not on the basis of "right" and "wrong," but on a sliding scale of values ranging from "not passable" to "outstanding." As a matter of fact, it is possible to achieve a relatively low score without a single "incorrect" answer because of evident weakness in the qualities being measured.

Occasionally, an examination may consist entirely of an oral test – either an individual or a group oral. In such cases, information is sought concerning the technical knowledges and abilities of the candidate, since there has been no written examination for this purpose. More commonly, however, an oral test is used to supplement a written examination.

Who conducts interviews?

The composition of oral boards varies among different jurisdictions. In nearly all, a representative of the personnel department serves as chairman. One of the members of the board may be a representative of the department in which the candidate would work. In some cases, "outside experts" are used, and, frequently, a businessman or some other representative of the general public is asked to serve. Labor and management or other special groups may be represented. The aim is to secure the services of experts in the appropriate field.

However the board is composed, it is a good idea (and not at all improper or unethical) to ascertain in advance of the interview who the members are and what groups they represent. When you are introduced to them, you will have some idea of their backgrounds and interests, and at least you will not stutter and stammer over their names.

What should be done before the interview?

While knowledge about the board members is useful and takes some of the surprise element out of the interview, there is other preparation which is more substantive. It *is* possible to prepare for an oral interview – in several ways:

1) Keep a copy of your application and review it carefully before the interview

This may be the only document before the oral board, and the starting point of the interview. Know what education and experience you have listed there, and the sequence and dates of all of it. Sometimes the board will ask you to review the highlights of your experience for them; you should not have to hem and haw doing it.

2) Study the class specification and the examination announcement

Usually, the oral board has one or both of these to guide them. The qualities, characteristics or knowledges required by the position sought are stated in these documents. They offer valuable clues as to the nature of the oral interview. For example, if the job involves supervisory responsibilities, the announcement will usually indicate that knowledge of modern supervisory methods and the qualifications of the candidate as a supervisor will be tested. If so, you can expect such questions, frequently in the form of a hypothetical situation which you are expected to solve. NEVER go into an oral without knowledge of the duties and responsibilities of the job you seek.

3) Think through each qualification required

Try to visualize the kind of questions you would ask if you were a board member. How well could you answer them? Try especially to appraise your own knowledge and background in each area, *measured against the job sought*, and identify any areas in which you are weak. Be critical and realistic – do not flatter yourself.

4) Do some general reading in areas in which you feel you may be weak

For example, if the job involves supervision and your past experience has NOT, some general reading in supervisory methods and practices, particularly in the field of human relations, might be useful. Do NOT study agency procedures or detailed manuals. The oral board will be testing your understanding and capacity, not your memory.

5) Get a good night's sleep and watch your general health and mental attitude

You will want a clear head at the interview. Take care of a cold or any other minor ailment, and of course, no hangovers.

What should be done on the day of the interview?

Now comes the day of the interview itself. Give yourself plenty of time to get there. Plan to arrive somewhat ahead of the scheduled time, particularly if your appointment is in the fore part of the day. If a previous candidate fails to appear, the board might be ready for you a bit early. By early afternoon an oral board is almost invariably behind schedule if there are many candidates, and you may have to wait. Take along a book or magazine to read, or your application to review, but leave any extraneous material in the waiting room when you go in for your interview. In any event, relax and compose yourself.

The matter of dress is important. The board is forming impressions about you – from your experience, your manners, your attitude, and your appearance. Give your personal appearance careful attention. Dress your best, but not your flashiest. Choose conservative, appropriate clothing, and be sure it is immaculate. This is a business interview, and your appearance should indicate that you regard it as such. Besides, being well groomed and properly dressed will help boost your confidence.

Sooner or later, someone will call your name and escort you into the interview room. *This is it.* From here on you are on your own. It is too late for any more preparation. But remember, you asked for this opportunity to prove your fitness, and you are here because your request was granted.

What happens when you go in?

The usual sequence of events will be as follows: The clerk (who is often the board stenographer) will introduce you to the chairman of the oral board, who will introduce you to the other members of the board. Acknowledge the introductions before you sit down. Do not be surprised if you find a microphone facing you or a stenotypist sitting by. Oral interviews are usually recorded in the event of an appeal or other review.

Usually the chairman of the board will open the interview by reviewing the highlights of your education and work experience from your application – primarily for the benefit of the other members of the board, as well as to get the material into the record. Do not interrupt or comment unless there is an error or significant misinterpretation; if that is the case, do not hesitate. But do not quibble about insignificant matters. Also, he will usually ask you some question about your education, experience or your present job – partly to get you to start talking and to establish the interviewing "rapport." He may start the actual questioning, or turn it over to one of the other members. Frequently, each member undertakes the questioning on a particular area, one in which he is perhaps most competent, so you can expect each member to participate in the examination. Because time is limited, you may also expect some rather abrupt switches in the direction the questioning takes, so do not be upset by it. Normally, a board member will not pursue a single line of questioning unless he discovers a particular strength or weakness.

After each member has participated, the chairman will usually ask whether any member has any further questions, then will ask you if you have anything you wish to add. Unless you are expecting this question, it may floor you. Worse, it may start you off on an extended, extemporaneous speech. The board is not usually seeking more information. The question is principally to offer you a last opportunity to present further qualifications or to indicate that you have nothing to add. So, if you feel that a significant qualification or characteristic has been overlooked, it is proper to point it out in a sentence or so. Do not compliment the board on the thoroughness of their examination – they have been sketchy, and you know it. If you wish, merely say, "No thank you, I have nothing further to add." This is a point where you can "talk yourself out" of a good impression or fail to present an important bit of information. Remember, *you close the interview yourself*.

The chairman will then say, "That is all, Mr. _____, thank you." Do not be startled; the interview is over, and quicker than you think. Thank him, gather your belongings and take your leave. Save your sigh of relief for the other side of the door.

How to put your best foot forward

Throughout this entire process, you may feel that the board individually and collectively is trying to pierce your defenses, seek out your hidden weaknesses and embarrass and confuse you. Actually, this is not true. They are obliged to make an appraisal of your qualifications for the job you are seeking, and they want to see you in your best light. Remember, they must interview all candidates and a non-cooperative candidate may become a failure in spite of their best efforts to bring out his qualifications. Here are 15 suggestions that will help you:

1) **Be natural – Keep your attitude confident, not cocky**

If you are not confident that you can do the job, do not expect the board to be. Do not apologize for your weaknesses, try to bring out your strong points. The board is interested in a positive, not negative, presentation. Cockiness will antagonize any board member and make him wonder if you are covering up a weakness by a false show of strength.

2) **Get comfortable, but don't lounge or sprawl**

Sit erectly but not stiffly. A careless posture may lead the board to conclude that you are careless in other things, or at least that you are not impressed by the importance of the occasion. Either conclusion is natural, even if incorrect. Do not fuss with your clothing, a pencil or an ashtray. Your hands may occasionally be useful to emphasize a point; do not let them become a point of distraction.

3) **Do not wisecrack or make small talk**

This is a serious situation, and your attitude should show that you consider it as such. Further, the time of the board is limited – they do not want to waste it, and neither should you.

4) Do not exaggerate your experience or abilities

In the first place, from information in the application or other interviews and sources, the board may know more about you than you think. Secondly, you probably will not get away with it. An experienced board is rather adept at spotting such a situation, so do not take the chance.

5) If you know a board member, do not make a point of it, yet do not hide it

Certainly you are not fooling him, and probably not the other members of the board. Do not try to take advantage of your acquaintanceship – it will probably do you little good.

6) Do not dominate the interview

Let the board do that. They will give you the clues – do not assume that you have to do all the talking. Realize that the board has a number of questions to ask you, and do not try to take up all the interview time by showing off your extensive knowledge of the answer to the first one.

7) Be attentive

You only have 20 minutes or so, and you should keep your attention at its sharpest throughout. When a member is addressing a problem or question to you, give him your undivided attention. Address your reply principally to him, but do not exclude the other board members.

8) Do not interrupt

A board member may be stating a problem for you to analyze. He will ask you a question when the time comes. Let him state the problem, and wait for the question.

9) Make sure you understand the question

Do not try to answer until you are sure what the question is. If it is not clear, restate it in your own words or ask the board member to clarify it for you. However, do not haggle about minor elements.

10) Reply promptly but not hastily

A common entry on oral board rating sheets is "candidate responded readily," or "candidate hesitated in replies." Respond as promptly and quickly as you can, but do not jump to a hasty, ill-considered answer.

11) Do not be peremptory in your answers

A brief answer is proper – but do not fire your answer back. That is a losing game from your point of view. The board member can probably ask questions much faster than you can answer them.

12) Do not try to create the answer you think the board member wants

He is interested in what kind of mind you have and how it works – not in playing games. Furthermore, he can usually spot this practice and will actually grade you down on it.

13) Do not switch sides in your reply merely to agree with a board member

Frequently, a member will take a contrary position merely to draw you out and to see if you are willing and able to defend your point of view. Do not start a debate, yet do not surrender a good position. If a position is worth taking, it is worth defending.

14) Do not be afraid to admit an error in judgment if you are shown to be wrong

The board knows that you are forced to reply without any opportunity for careful consideration. Your answer may be demonstrably wrong. If so, admit it and get on with the interview.

15) Do not dwell at length on your present job

The opening question may relate to your present assignment. Answer the question but do not go into an extended discussion. You are being examined for a *new* job, not your present one. As a matter of fact, try to phrase ALL your answers in terms of the job for which you are being examined.

Basis of Rating

Probably you will forget most of these "do's" and "don'ts" when you walk into the oral interview room. Even remembering them all will not ensure you a passing grade. Perhaps you did not have the qualifications in the first place. But remembering them will help you to put your best foot forward, without treading on the toes of the board members.

Rumor and popular opinion to the contrary notwithstanding, an oral board wants you to make the best appearance possible. They know you are under pressure – but they also want to see how you respond to it as a guide to what your reaction would be under the pressures of the job you seek. They will be influenced by the degree of poise you display, the personal traits you show and the manner in which you respond.

ABOUT THIS BOOK

This book contains tests divided into Examination Sections. Go through each test, answering every question in the margin. We have also attached a sample answer sheet at the back of the book that can be removed and used. At the end of each test look at the answer key and check your answers. On the ones you got wrong, look at the right answer choice and learn. Do not fill in the answers first. Do not memorize the questions and answers, but understand the answer and principles involved. On your test, the questions will likely be different from the samples. Questions are changed and new ones added. If you understand these past questions you should have success with any changes that arise. Tests may consist of several types of questions. We have additional books on each subject should more study be advisable or necessary for you. Finally, the more you study, the better prepared you will be. This book is intended to be the last thing you study before you walk into the examination room. Prior study of relevant texts is also recommended. NLC publishes some of these in our Fundamental Series. Knowledge and good sense are important factors in passing your exam. Good luck also helps. So now study this Passbook, absorb the material contained within and take that knowledge into the examination. Then do your best to pass that exam.

EXAMINATION SECTION

EXAMINATION SECTION
TEST 1

DIRECTIONS: Each question or incomplete statement is followed by several suggested answers or completions. Select the one that BEST answers the question or completes the statement. *PRINT THE LETTER OF THE CORRECT ANSWER IN THE SPACE AT THE RIGHT.*

1. The allowance for doubtful accounts represents the

    A. difference between the gross value of accounts receivable and the net realizable value of accounts receivable
    B. amount of uncollectible accounts written off to date
    C. difference between total credit sales and collection on credit sales
    D. cash set aside to compensate for bad debt losses

    1.____

2. What is the term for the interest deducted from the face amount of a note payable?

    A. Discount
    B. Fee
    C. Levy
    D. Contingency

    2.____

3. The Yardman purchases a mower from an equipment dealer on February 1 for $7,200. The dealer has guaranteed the mower to have a useful life of 10 years. Assuming adjusting entries are prepared monthly, the book value of the mower on June 30 is

    A. $300
    B. $6480
    C. $6900
    D. $7,200

    3.____

4. Gullstart, Inc. had operating cash flows of $240,000, total cash flows of $1 million, and average total assets of $5 million. Its cash flow on total assets ratio is

    A. 3.6%
    B. 4.8%
    C. 5.0%
    D. 12.4%

    4.____

5. Which of the following assets would NOT be depreciated?

    A. Buildings
    B. Servers/information systems
    C. Land
    D. Store fixtures

    5.____

Questions 6-8 refer to the following information: On January 1, five years ago, Winkler and Dunnebier Machinery purchased an envelope machine for $1.5 million. The machine was given a useful life of 5 years or 40,000 hours. During the machine's 5-year life span, its hourly usage was, respectively, 4000; 8000; 16,000,; 10,000; and 2000 hours.

6. Using the double-declining balance method, calculate the depreciation expense for the FIRST year.

   A. $135,000
   B. $360,000
   C. $540,000
   D. $600,000

6.____

7. Using the units-of-production method, calculate the depreciation expense for the THIRD year.

   A. $129,600
   B. $216,000
   C. $337,500
   D. $540,000

7.____

8. Using the straight-line method, calculate the depreciation expense for the FIFTH year.

   A. $44,400
   B. $67,500
   C. $270,000
   D. $360,000

8.____

9. The _____ principle requires expenses to be reported in the same period as the revenues the were earned as a result of the expenses.

   A. realization
   B. cost
   C. matching
   D. going-concern

9.____

10. To recognize insurance expired during an accounting period, the adjusting entry will affect the _____ account.
    I.   asset
    II. expense
    III. liability
    IV. revenue

    A. I and II
    B. II and III
    C. III and IV
    D. I, II, III and IV

10.____

11. Adjusting entries for annual financial statements are generally made

    A. at the beginning of the year
    B. after every transaction
    C. periodically throughout the year
    D. at the end of the year

11.____

12. In a ledger, debit entries

    A. decrease assets
    B. increase owners' equity

12.____

C. decrease liabilities
D. decrease profitability

13. What is the term for a person who signs a note receivable and promises to pay the principal and interest? 13.____

    A. Payee
    B. Holder
    C. Maker
    D. Recipient

14. Trusty, Inc. had net credit sales for the year of $120,000. Accounts receivable at year's end are $40,000, and there is a $200 credit in allowance for doubtful accounts. If Trusty estimates bad debt losses based on an aging of accounts receivable as $2400, the expense for the year is 14.____

    A. $200
    B. $2200
    C. $2400
    D. $2600

15. When bonds are issued at a discount, the discount 15.____

    A. appears on the balance sheet as a contra liability
    B. reduces the overall cost of borrowing
    C. appears on the income statement as other income
    D. appears on the income statement as an expense

16. Dividends become a liability on the date that 16.____

    A. the dividend is declared by the board of directors
    B. the dividend is recorded
    C. cumulative preferred stock dividends are declared in arrears
    D. payment of the dividends is made

17. The financial statement of a large corporation is MOST likely to include 17.____

    A. book value per share
    B. earnings per share
    C. the current ratio
    D. return on assets

18. _____ are long-term notes issued with a pledge of specified property, plant, and equipment for the loan. 18.____

    A. sinking-fund bonds
    B. mortgage notes payable
    C. bonds payable
    D. foreclosures

19. Empire Waste sold a truck that originally cost $200,000 for $120,000. The accumulated depreciation on the truck was $80,000. Empire Waste should record a   19._____

   A. $40,000 loss
   B. $40,000 gain
   C. $80,000 loss
   D. break-even transaction

20. The "chart of accounts" refers to a   20._____

   A. complete listing of the account titles to be used
   B. collection of all a company's accounts
   C. system of recording debit and credit entries for each transaction
   D. statement that shows the name and balance of all ledger accounts

21. If net credit sales for a given year are $800,000 and the average accounts receivable are $40,000, the accounts receivable turnover is   21._____

   A. 20
   B. 50
   C. 80
   D. 100

22. During a period of steadily rising prices, the _____ method of inventory valuation is likely to result in the lowest cost of goods sold.   22._____

   A. gross profit
   B. last in, first out (LIFO)
   C. first in, first out (FIFO)
   D. specific identification

23. On an income statement, each of the following would appear below income from continuing operations, EXCEPT   23._____

   A. discontinued operations
   B. net income
   C. extraordinary items
   D. cumulative effect of accounting changes related to previous years

24. During the month of December, the liabilities of Duckworth increased $26,000 and the owners' equity decreased $6000. The assets of Duckworth _____ during December.   24._____

   A. increased $20,000
   B. increased $22,000
   C. decreased $20,000
   D. decreased $32,000

25. At year's end, Lavender, Inc. is estimating its ending inventory. The following information is available:

Inventory as of October 1 $ 12,500
Net fourth-quarter sales $40,000
Net fourth-quarter purchases $27,500

Lavender typically achieves a gross profit of around 15%. Using the gross profit method, calculate Lavender's ending inventory.

A. $4000
B. $6000
C. $10,000
D. $16,000

KEY (CORRECT ANSWERS)

1.	A	11.	D
2.	A	12.	C
3.	C	13.	C
4.	B	14.	B
5.	C	15.	A
6.	D	16.	A
7.	D	17.	B
8.	C	18.	B
9.	C	19.	D
10.	A	20.	A

21. A
22. C
23. D
24. A
25. B

TEST 2

DIRECTIONS: Each question or incomplete statement is followed by several suggested answers or completions. Select the one that BEST answers the question or completes the statement. *PRINT THE LETTER OF THE CORRECT ANSWER IN THE SPACE AT THE RIGHT.*

1. Which of the following is a balance sheet item that represents the portion of stockholders' equity resulting form profitable business operation?

    A. Retained earnings
    B. Cash
    C. Accounts receivable
    D. Capital stock

    1.____

2. Which of the following is sued to compare revenues and expenses for a period of time in order to determine net income or loss?

    A. Balance sheet
    B. Owners' equity statement
    C. Statement of cash flows
    D. Income statement

    2.____

3. Accounting transactions are first recorded in the

    A. ledger
    B. trial balance
    C. journal
    D. T-account

    3.____

4. If net credit sales for a given year are $1.2 million and the average accounts receivable is $120,000, the average days to collect receivables is

    A. 10
    B. 30
    C. 36.5
    D. 71

    4.____

5. Each of the following is included in an end-of-period worksheet, EXCEPT

    A. financial statement information
    B. closing entries
    C. trial balance
    D. information for adjusting entries

    5.____

6. Generally accepted accounting principles suggest that a company's balance sheet show assets as the

    A. market value of the asset received in all cases
    B. cash equivalent value of what was given up or the asset received, whichever is more evident
    C. objective cost of external users
    D. cash outlay only, even if part of the consideration given was something other than cash

    6.____

7. At the end of the accounting period, Tripod Industries failed to make an adjusting entry to record depreciation. The effect of this omission will be an

   A. understatement of expenses
   B. understatement of assets
   C. overstatement of liabilities
   D. overstatement of revenues

8. On October 1, Agitpro paid three months' rent for office space. The payment was originally recorded in prepaid rent. Agitpro's adjusting entry on October 31 would include a

   A. debit to rent payable
   B. credit to rent expense
   C. debit to prepaid rent
   D. credit to prepaid rent

9. Beulah's Salon purchased a hair dryer on January 1 for $5,400. The dryer has a useful life of 10 years and a salvage value of $400. Using the double-declining balance method, calculate the depreciation expense for the second year of the dryer's useful life.

   A. $628
   B. $800
   C. $864
   D. $1026

10. The face amount of a bond, plus the unamortized premium, is referred to as its _____ value.

    A. carrying
    B. discounted
    C. par
    D. adjusted

11. Metabolon has a $10,000 credit balance in its allowance for doubtful accounts. During October it wrote off $4000 as uncollectible from a bankrupt customer. This entry will

    A. reduce owners' equity
    B. not affect the net income for the period
    C. increase total assets
    D. reduce total assets

12. A company uses a perpetual inventory system. When goods sold have been returned, the company should record the return with a

    A. debit to sales returns and allowances
    B. credit to inventory
    C. debit to cost of goods sold
    D. credit to sales returns and allowances

13. The objectives of financial reporting are met largely by each of the following, EXCEPT the

    A. cash flow statement
    B. federal income tax return

C. income statement
D. statement of financial position

14. _____ entries are used to zero out the balance in nominal accounts at the end of the period.

   A. Reversing
   B. Real
   C. Closing
   D. Adjusting

15. On October 1, Sterling Enterprises borrowed $100,000 from the bank. The loan is to be repaid in total in six months. The interest rate is 9%. On November 30, Sterling's total liability for this loan will be

   A. $100,000
   B. $101,500
   C. $104,500
   D. $109,000

16. Which of the following is shown on a bank statement?
   I. Deposits in transit
   II. Beginning and ending balances of the depositor's checking ac count
   III. Petty cash amounts
   IV. Outstanding checks

   A. I and II
   B. II only
   C. I, II and IV
   D. I, II, III and IV

17. Navanax had 25,000 shares of 8% preferred stock, $100 par, and 250,000 shares of $1 par common stock outstanding throughout the year. Net income for the year was $1,100,000, and Navanax declared and distributed a cash dividend of $2 per share on its common stock. Earnings per share equaled

   A. $1.60
   B. $2.10
   C. $3.60
   D. $4.40

18. A 120-day note, dated March 25, has a maturity date of July

   A. 22
   B. 23
   C. 24
   D. 25

19. Of the following steps in the accounting cycle, which is performed FIRST?

   A. Adjusting accounts
   B. Preparing an adjusted trial balance
   C. Posting
   D. Closing temporary accounts

Questions 20 and 21 refer to the following information: On March 1, Richie Corporation bought land by signing a note payable to the bank.

20. The March 1 journal entry would include a debit to the _____ account.   20._____

    A. revenue
    B. owners' equity
    C. liability
    D. asset

21. The March 1 journal entry would include a credit to the _____ account.   21._____

    A. liability
    B. asset
    C. owners' equity
    D. expense

22. A company's _____ activities are transactions with creditors to borrow money and/or   22._____
    repay the principal amounts of loans reported as cash flows.

    A. leveraging
    B. financing
    C. investing
    D. operating

23. Under the direct write-off method of accounting for uncollectible assets,   23._____

    A. the matching principle is illustrated by the relationship between current period net sales and current period uncollectible accounts
    B. when specific accounts receivable are determined to be worthless, the allowance for doubtful accounts is debited
    C. accounts receivable are not recorded in the balance sheet at net realizable value, but in the balance of the accounts receivable ledger account
    D. the uncollectible accounts expense is less than the expense would be under the income statement approach

24. The true interest rate of a note, computed only on the remaining balance of the unpaid   24._____
    debt for the specific time period, is known as the _____ interest rate.

    A. adjusted
    B. annual effective
    C. net
    D. annual compounded

25. An accountant is using the indirect method to calculate and report the net cash provided   25._____
    or used by operating activities. Under this method the accountant will have to adjust net income for

    I. revenues and expenses that did not provide or use cash
    II. changes in noncash current assets and current liabilities related to operating activities
    III. changes in current liabilities related to operating activities
    IV. gains and losses from investing and financing activities

A. I and II
B. I, II and III
C. II, III and IV
D. I, II, III and IV

KEY (CORRECT ANSWERS)

1.	A	11.	B
2.	D	12.	A
3.	C	13.	B
4.	C	14.	C
5.	B	15.	B
6.	B	16.	B
7.	A	17.	C
8.	D	18.	B
9.	C	19.	A
10.	A	20.	D

21. A
22. C
23. C
24. B
25. D

TEST 3

DIRECTIONS: Each question or incomplete statement is followed by several suggested answers or completions. Select the one that BEST answers the question or completes the statement. *PRINT THE LETTER OF THE CORRECT ANSWER IN THE SPACE AT THE RIGHT.*

1. An accountant is using the allowance method of recording bad debts. The journal entry to record the bad debts adjustment would

    A. debit the allowance for doubtful accounts
    B. credit the allowance for doubtful accounts
    C. debit accounts receivable
    D. credit accounts receivable

    1._____

2. The primary consumers of financial accounting information are

    A. investors and creditors
    B. corporate boards of directors
    C. financial managers
    D. budget officers

    2._____

3. The balance sheet of Fred's Fancies, a retailer, includes equipment, accounts receivable, cash, accounts payable, supplies, capital stock, notes payable, and notes receivable. This balance sheet contains _____ assets and _____ liabilities.

    A. 5; 2
    B. 5; 3
    C. 4; 4
    D. 6; 1

    3._____

4. The cost principle requires assets such as land, buildings, and equipment be recorded at

    A. appraisal value at the time of purchase
    B. appraisal value at the balance sheet date
    C. historical cost
    D. fair market value

    4._____

5. Each of the following would affect the book side of a bank reconciliation, EXCEPT

    A. a bank debit memorandum
    B. bank service charges
    C. outstanding checks
    D. a check-printing fee from the bank

    5._____

6. Ichthys Dive Shops borrowed $300,000 cash from the bank by signing a 5-year, 8% installment note. Given that the present value factor of an 8% annuity for 5 years is 3.9927 and each payment is $75,137, the present value of the note is

    A. $75,137
    B. $94,013
    C. $300,000
    D. $375,685

    6._____

7. Before any year-end adjusting entries were made, the Tansu Mill's net income was $40,000. The following adjustments need to be made:

Portion of insurance expiring	$300
Interest accrued on company savings	$110
Fees collected in advance now earned	$2,400

   The income statement for the current year should show a net income of

   A. $37,410
   B. $38,010
   C. $41,990
   D. $42,210

8. If a substantial amount of a company's accounts payable are paid in cash, the company's current ratio would

   A. increase
   B. decrease
   C. remain the same
   D. change depending on the relationship between the payables and the current liabilities

9. Superscrubbers began providing janitorial services for a large corporation on January 15 for a monthly fee of $10,000. The first payment is to be received on February 15. The adjusting entry made by Superscrubbers on January 31 includes a

   A. debit of $5000 to janitorial fees receivable
   B. credit of $5000 to janitorial fees earned
   C. credit of $10,000 to janitorial fees earned
   D. debit of $5000 to unearned janitorial fees

10. Which of the following would NOT be closed during the closing process?

    A. Advertising expense
    B. Dividends
    C. Interest revenue
    D. Accumulated depreciation

11. The _____ principle requires that every business be accounted for separately and distinctly from its owner or owners.

    A. realization
    B. objectivity
    C. business entity
    D. compartmentalization

12. Funky Chic Decorating purchased a window treatment display for $25,000 and sold it several years later for $12,000. The original estimated residual value was $10,000, and the accumulated depreciation at the time of sale was $8000. The sale should be recorded as a

    A. $3000 loss
    B. $5000 loss

C. $2000 gain
D. $3000 gain

13. During a period of falling prices, the _____ method of inventory valuation will generally result in the highest amount of income taxes paid.

   A. first in, first out (FIFO)
   B. last in, first out (LIFO)
   C. gross profit
   D. weighted average

14. Which of the following statements about retained earnings is FALSE?

   A. They are not subject to statutory restrictions.
   B. They usually approximate a company's cumulative net income less dividends declared.
   C. They may be subject to appropriations by corporate directors for the purpose of limiting dividends.
   D. They may be subject to restrictions due to loan agreements.

15. On August 11 of the current year, Trachtenberg Corporation concluded that a customer's $8700 account receivable was uncollectible, and wrote the account off. Assuming the allowance method is used to account for bad debts, the write-off will

   A. have no effect on either net income or total assets
   B. decrease net income, but have no effect on total assets
   C. have no effect on net income, but decrease total assets
   D. decrease both net income and total assets

16. Chuzzlewit Enterprises sold equipment for $30,000. The cost was $70,000, and the equipment had accumulated depreciation of $50,000 at the time of the sale. In the investing section of the cash flow statement, the amount of _____ would be entered for this transaction.

   A. $0 (no entry)
   B. $10,000
   C. $20,000
   D. $30,000

Questions 17-19 refer to the following information: Multiplastics purchased a machine in January 1 that cost $300,000, has a residual value of $20,000, and a useful life of seven years.

17. The amount of depreciation expense for the second year, under the double-declining balance method, would be

   A. $47,287
   B. $53,576
   C. $61,261
   D. $85,800

18. The amount of depreciation expense for the third year, under the sum-of-the-years'-digits method, would be

A. $50,000
B. $53,576
C. $63,567
D. $70,000

19. The net book value of the machine at the end of the fourth year (after recording fourth-year depreciation), using the straight-line method, would be

   A. $120,000
   B. $140,000
   C. $171,429
   D. $188,888

20. The purpose of a classified balance sheet is to

   A. organize assets and liabilities into important subgroups
   B. show revenues, expenses, and net income
   C. report operating, investing, and financing activities
   D. measure a company's ability to pay its bills in a timely manner

21. What is the term for an expense resulting from a failure to take advantage of cash discounts on purchases?

   A. Trade discounts
   B. Shortfall
   C. Sales discounts
   D. Discounts lost

22. Accounts that appear on a postclosing trial balance are referred to as _____ accounts.

   A. projected
   B. real
   C. prorata
   D. nominal

23. Which of the following is an example of an operating activity?

   A. Purchasing office equipment
   B. Paying wages
   C. Selling stock
   D. Borrowing money from a bank

24. Landshark Corporation has operated with a gross profit rate of 30% for the last several years. On January 1 of the current year the company had an inventory with a cost of $50,000. Purchases of merchandise during January amounted to $60,000, and sales for the month were $90,000. Using the gross profit method, the estimated inventory on January 31 is

   A. $27,000
   B. $47,000
   C. $59,000
   D. $63,000

25. Earnings per share is an accounting item that is 25.____
- A. optional for most companies
- B. shown on the face of the income statement
- C. computed for both preferred and common stock
- D. expressed as "return on equity" in the ledger

KEY (CORRECT ANSWERS)

1.	A	11.	C
2.	A	12.	B
3.	A	13.	B
4.	C	14.	A
5.	C	15.	A
6.	C	16.	D
7.	D	17.	C
8.	A	18.	A
9.	B	19.	B
10.	D	20.	A

21.	D
22.	B
23.	B
24.	B
25.	B

TEST 4

DIRECTIONS: Each question or incomplete statement is followed by several suggested answers or completions. Select the one that BEST answers the question or completes the statement. *PRINT THE LETTER OF THE CORRECT ANSWER IN THE SPACE AT THE RIGHT.*

1. After the Yan Company collects $10,000 of its notes receivable, total assets are

    A. increased by $10,000
    B. decreased by $10,000
    C. unchanged, but total liabilities are greater
    D. unchanged

2. Revenues, expenses, and owner's withdrawal accounts are examples of _____ accounts.

    A. real
    B. permanent
    C. temporary
    D. closing

3. At the end of the year, the owners' equity of Plebeian Enterprises is $240,000, and is equal to 75% of total liabilities. The amount of total assets is

    A. $80,000
    B. $320,000
    C. $420,000
    D. $560,000

4. The _____ ratio of a company shows the percent of total assets provided by creditors.

    A. total asset turnover
    B. acid
    C. return on total assets
    D. debt

5. Which of the following would be recorded as a current liability?

    A. Accrued wages payable
    B. Property taxes payable
    C. Vacation benefits
    D. Income taxes payable

Questions 6-9 refer to the following information:
Year-end inventory for the Standish Company, under the periodic inventory system, is $25,000. The inventory on the first day of the year was $20,000 and purchases made during the year cost $40,000. Purchase returns and allowances equaled $1500, transportation in cost $500, and net sales for the year totaled $75,000.

6. At year's end, the net cost of purchases for Standish was

    A. $38,500
    B. $39,000

C. $40,000
D. $40,500

7. At year's end, the cost of goods sold for Standish was

   A. $31,500
   B. $34,000
   C. $44,000
   D. $59,000

8. At year's end, the cost of goods available for sale for Standish was

   A. $34,000
   B. $44,000
   C. $59,000
   D. $64,000

9. At year's end, the gross margin on sales for Standish was

   A. $41,000
   B. $44,000
   C. $59,000
   D. $61,000

10. Which of the following is a common nonrecurring item on the income statement?

    A. Discontinued operations
    B. Operating income
    C. Cumulative effect of a change in accounting estimate
    D. Ordinary gains and losses

11. If a transaction causes an asset account to decrease, it may also result in an increase

    A. in the combined total of liabilities and stockholders' equity
    B. of an equal amount in another asset account
    C. in a liability account
    D. of an equal amount in a stockholders' equity account

12. Beverly Corp. had total operating expenses of $100,000 in the previous accounting period; depreciation of $2,000; and an increase in accrued liabilities of $5,000. The company's prepaid expenses at the beginning of the period were $18,000; at the ending, they were $12,000.

    What was the cash paid by Beverly Corp. for operating expenses?

    A. $87,000
    B. $91,000
    C. $99,000
    D. $101,000

13. The _____ method of inventory valuation identifies the invoice cost of each item in ending inventory to determine the cost assigned to that inventory.

A. specific identification
B. first in, first out (FIFO)
C. last in, first out (LIFO)
D. weighted-average

14. In which of the following situations would revenue be recognized?

    A. An order is received with cash payment, and the order will be filled next month.
    B. An order has been shipped and will arrive at the customer's place of business after the end of the month. Shipping terms are FOB destination.
    C. An order has been received, and the goods have been set aside for the customer to pick up at her convenience.
    D. An order is received, and it will take about a week to manufacture enough goods to fill it.

15. A credit is used to record a(n)

    A. increase in an asset
    B. decrease in an expense
    C. increase in a liability
    D. increase in owners' equity

16. To balance the income statement columns of a worksheet, net income should be entered in the

    A. adjustments debit column
    B. balance sheet debit column
    C. income statement debit column
    D. income statement credit column

17. On May 1, Horticopia's accounts receivable totaled $6000. The allowance for doubtful accounts was $240. During the month of May, Horticopia made $20,000 in credit sales and collected $19,600 from its customers. On May 31, the not realizable value of accounts receivable is

    A. $6000
    B. $6160
    C. $6400
    D. $6640

18. Which of the following would affect the bank side of a bank reconciliation?

    A. Interest earned on a checking account
    B. Bank service charges
    C. Bank credit memorandum
    D. Deposits in transit

19. _____ preferred stock is a kind of stock on which the right to receive dividends is forfeited for any year in which dividends are not declared.

    A. Convertible
    B. Callable
    C. Noncumulative
    D. Cumulative

20. Which of the following are trade receivables?

    A. Deposits with creditors
    B. Cash advances to employees
    C. Amounts owed by customers on account
    D. Loans to affiliated companies

21. Which of the following is a term for the accounting procedure that estimates and reports bad debts expense from credit sales during the period of the sales, and also reports accounts receivable at the amount of cash proceeds that is expected from their collection?

    A. Adjustment method for uncollectible debts
    B. Aging of notes receivable
    C. Direct write-off method of accounting for bad debts
    D. Allowance method of accounting for bad debts

22. If Floracom accrues $200,000 for salaries payable at the end of the year,

    A. assets and owners' equity will remain unchanged
    B. assets decrease and liabilities increase by $200,000
    C. liabilities decrease and owners' equity increases by $200,000
    D. liabilities and expenses each increase $200,000

23. Each of the following is an operating activity, EXCEPT

    A. the purchase of equipment for cash
    B. the purchase of supplies for cash
    C. interest paid on a note payable
    D. cash sale

24. Compared to a perpetual inventory system, a periodic inventory system

    A. provides more timely information
    B. is based on estimates
    C. requires updating inventory-related accounts only at the end of each period
    D. allows a company to determine inventory and cost of goods sold at any time

25. On January 1, Uniqual Inc. purchased a machine for $60,000. The machine is estimated to have a useful life of 5 years and a salvage value of $10,000. Using the double-declining balance method of depreciation, what is the book value of the asset at the end of the year?

    A. $21,600
    B. $32,000
    C. $38,400
    D. $48,000

KEY (CORRECT ANSWERS)

1. D
2. C
3. D
4. D
5. A

6. B
7. B
8. C
9. A
10. A

11. B
12. A
13. A
14. C
15. B

16. C
17. B
18. D
19. C
20. C

21. D
22. D
23. A
24. C
25. A

EXAMINATION SECTION
TEST 1

DIRECTIONS: Each question or incomplete statement is followed by several suggested answers or completions. Select the one that BEST answers the question or completes the statement. *PRINT THE LETTER OF THE CORRECT ANSWER IN THE SPACE AT THE RIGHT.*

1. At the end of the year, Obama Motors failed to make an adjusting entry to record the interest accrued on a note payable. As a result, the

    A. current assets were overstated
    B. owners' equity was understated
    C. current ratio was understated
    D. working capital was overstated

1.____

2. For a retail business, the difference between net sales revenue and cost of goods sold is expressed as

    A. net operating margin
    B. net income
    C. operating expense
    D. gross margin

2.____

3. The disposal of long-term assets is classified as a(n) _____ activity.

    A. planning
    B. financing
    C. operating
    D. investing

3.____

4. During a period of falling prices, the _____ method of inventory valuation will generally result in the highest cost of goods sold

    A. first in, first out (FIFO)
    B. last in, first out (LIFO)
    C. weighted average
    D. specific identification

4.____

5. Which of the following are NOT cash equivalents?

    A. U.S. Treasury bills
    B. Guaranteed investment contracts
    C. Accounts receivable due in ten days
    D. Money market accounts

5.____

6. An adjusting entry to record interest that has accrued on a not payable to the bank will cause an immediate

    A. reduction in net income and increase in liabilities
    B. reduction in net income and decrease in liabilities
    C. reduction in net income and decrease in assets
    D. increase in net income and increase in assets

6.____

7. An April 30 trial balance, before adjustments, shows office supplies of $600 and office supplies expenses of $1010. An April adjusting entry recorded office supplies expense of $170. After the April adjusting entries are made, the office supplies account balance for April 30 will be

   A. $430
   B. $770
   C. $840
   D. $1180

8. Ogee Masonry uses a perpetual inventory system. At the beginning of the year, inventory was $50,000. During the year, Ogee bought merchandise for $230,000 and sold merchandise costing $245,000. A year-end physical inventory indicated shrinkage losses of $4,000. Before recording these shrinkage losses, Ogee's inventory balance is

   A. $31,000
   B. $35,000
   C. $42,000
   D. $50,000

9. Adjusting entries are NOT required for

   A. accrual basis accounting
   B. inventory
   C. the matching principle
   D. cash basis accounting

10. Bob Eyans has a net income of $44,000; operating income of $100,000; sales of $400,000; and interest expense of $4000. What is Bob Evans' interest coverage ratio?

    A. 10
    B. 11
    C. 22.7
    D. 25

11. The Stearns Group had a taxable income of $8000 in the current year. The MACRS depreciation was $3000 while the income statement reported depreciation of $1000. Assuming no other differences between tax and accounting income, The Stearns Group's pretax accounting income was

    A. $4000
    B. $5000
    C. $10,000
    D. $11,000

12. Accounts receivable typically appear on the

    A. balance sheet
    B. income statement
    C. statement of cash flows
    D. statement of retained earnings

13. A plant asset can no longer be used to produce goods with a competitive advantage, because of new innovations and improvements. The asset is described as

    A. depleted
    B. amortized
    C. inadequate
    D. obsolescent

13.____

Questions 14 and 15 refer to the following information: On July 4, the owners of Vanguard invested $500,000 and received shares of common stock.

14. The July 4 journal entry would include a debit to the _____ account.

    A. liability
    B. asset
    C. owners' equity
    D. expense

14.____

15. The July 4 journal entry would include a credit to the _____ account.

    A. owners' equity
    B. revenue
    C. expense
    D. liability

15.____

16. The total amount of stock that a corporation's charter allows it to issue is referred to as _____ stock.

    A. preferred
    B. authorized
    C. common
    D. finite

16.____

17. When companies use assets or incur liabilities when earning revenues, they incur a(n)

    A. expense
    B. liability
    C. revenue
    D. owners' equity

17.____

18. _____ show each financial statement item in relation to a financial statement total.

    A. General-purpose financial statements
    B. Common-size statements
    C. Horizontal analyses
    D. Vertical analyses

18.____

19. In the long term, the most important inflows of cash should come from

    A. operating activities
    B. creditors
    C. investing activities
    D. stock sales

19.____

20. Which of the following would be recorded as an intangible asset?   20.____

    A. Buildings used in business operations
    B. Patents
    C. Office Supplies
    D. Accounts receivable

21. Bionix Corporation issued a 13%, 90-day, $12,000 note payable bearing interest on the   21.____
    face amount dated August 1, 2001. AT maturity, Bionix should record the payment of the
    note with the following:

    A. $13,560 debit to notes payable; $13,560 credit to cash
    B. $ 12,390 debit to notes payable; $ 12,390 credit to cash
    C. $ 12,000 debit to notes payable; $ 12,000 credit to cash
    D. $ 12,000 debit to notes payable; $390 debit to interest expense; $ 12,390 credit to
       cash

22. Which of the following is a typical cash flow from operating activities?   22.____

    A. Repayment of loan principal
    B. Proceeds from bond issues
    C. Receipts of cash sales
    D. Proceeds from collecting loan principal

23. What is the term used to refer to the periodic allocation of the costs of intangible assets   23.____
    to expense?

    A. Depletion
    B. Depreciation
    C. Accrual
    D. Amortization

24. An accountant discovers $282 in extra cash at the end of the day. The proper entry for   24.____
    this would include a

    A. debit to expense
    B. credit to cash
    C. debit to petty cash
    D. credit to cash over and short

25. Blue Ivonk Enterprises uses the periodic inventory system. Over the past year, it earned   25.____
    a gross profit margin of 40% on $80,000 in sales. Its beginning inventory was valued at
    $20,000 and it made $100,000 in purchases. The cost of sales value over the past year
    was

    A. $32,000
    B. $40,000
    C. $48,000
    D. $50,000

KEY (CORRECT ANSWERS)

1.	D	11.	C
2.	D	12.	A
3.	D	13.	D
4.	A	14.	B
5.	C	15.	A
6.	A	16.	B
7.	A	17.	A
8.	B	18.	D
9.	D	19.	A
10.	D	20.	B

21. D
22. C
23. D
24. D
25. C

TEST 2

DIRECTIONS: Each question or incomplete statement is followed by several suggested answers or completions. Select the one that BEST answers the question or completes the statement. *PRINT THE LETTER OF THE CORRECT ANSWER IN THE SPACE AT THE RIGHT.*

1. An estimated liability is most accurately described as a(n) 1.____

    A. unknown liability of a certain amount
    B. known liability of an uncertain amount
    C. liability whose amount is not recorded until its amount is known for certain
    D. liability that may occur as the result of a future event

2. The debt ratio is a measure of 2.____

    A. long-term risk
    B. short-term solvency
    C. profitability
    D. net cash flows from financing activities

3. A six-month, 12% note receivable for $600,000 was received from a customer on September 2. The adjustment to interest receivable on December 31 would be 3.____

    A. $12,000
    B. $24,000
    C. $36,000
    D. $72,000

4. A net operating loss's effect on taxes is usually _____ at the end of the net operating loss year. 4.____

    A. subject to a valuation allowance
    B. expressed as a deferred tax liability
    C. shown as a current receivable
    D. expressed as a deferred tax asset

5. When preparing a bank reconciliation, checks outstanding would 5.____

    A. decrease the bank balance
    B. increase the bank balance
    C. decrease the book balance
    D. increase the book balance

Questions 6-8 refer to the information below.

During the month of September, Benedict Life recorded the following transactions:

Cash received from bank loans	$5000
Revenues earned and received in cash	$4500
Expenses incurred and paid	$2500
Dividends paid to stockholders in cash	$2000

6. Net cash flows from Benedict Life's operating activities for September were   6._____

   A. $0
   B. $2000
   C. $4500
   D. $7000

7. The amount of net income reported on the September income statement will be   7._____

   A. $2000
   B. $2500
   C. $4500
   D. $5000

8. At the beginning of September, stockholders' equity in Benedict Life was $60,000. At the end of the month, it was   8._____

   A. $58,000
   B. $60,000
   C. $62,000
   D. $64,500

9. Under the direct method of reporting cash used in operating activities, the reconciliation of net income to cash provided by operating activities is recorded   9._____

   A. in a supplemental schedule to the statement of cash flows
   B. at the end of the statement of cash flows
   C. at the beginning of the statement of cash flows
   D. on the face of the statement of cash flows

10. Which of the following does NOT strengthen internal control over cash receipts?   10._____

    A. The daily bank deposit of cash receipts intact
    B. A cash register
    C. A daily listing of all checks received by mail
    D. A voucher system

11. What is the term for a statement that shows the name and balance of all ledger accounts, arranged according to whether they are debits or credits?   11._____

    A. General ledger
    B. Journal
    C. Trial balance
    D. Chart of accounts

12. Fees earned typically appear on the   12._____

    A. statement of retained earnings
    B. balance sheet
    C. statement of cash flows
    D. income statement

13. Goods in transit are included in a purchaser's inventory   13.____

    A. if the goods are shipped free-on-board
    B. after the goods have traveled halfway between seller and purchaser
    C. when the purchaser is responsible for paying freight charges
    D. during any time they are in transit

14. Starmont Bakery, which has an adequate amount in its allowance for doubtful accounts, writes off an account receivable from a bankrupt customer as uncollectible. The result will be that   14.____

    A. gross accounts receivable will decrease
    B. owners' equity will increase
    C. total current assets will increase
    D. total current assets will decrease

15. Depletion is determined in a way that is similar to the _____ method of depreciation.   15.____

    A. sum-of-the-years'-digits
    B. double declining balance
    C. production unit
    D. straighline

16. It's December 31, 2015, and Anton Fields Corporation is conducting its end-of-year accounting. Which of the following would NOT be a current liability for the company?   16.____

    A. The portion of long-term debt due in 2016
    B. Warranty liability for products carrying a two-year warranty and sold during 2015
    C. Interest due to creditors and bondholders for 2016, to be paid in 2016
    D. Consulting fees collected in advance in 2015, to be collected in 2016

17. Junket Travel received cash proceeds of $408,777 on a bond issue with a par value of $400,000. The difference between the par value and the issue price would be recorded as a   17.____

    A. credit to premium on bonds payable
    B. debit to premium on bonds payable
    C. credit to discount on bonds payable
    D. debit to discount on bonds payable

18. Ledgertnax calls for a 2-for-1 stock split. A stockholder who owns 200 shares of the stock before the split will own _____ shares after the split.   18.____

    A. 100
    B. 200
    C. 400
    D. 600

19. Which of the following occurs when a corporation receives donated capital?   19.____

    A. A gain is recognized.
    B. The asset is recorded at the donor's cost.
    C. The donor receives a tax deduction.
    D. The asset is recorded at fair market value.

20. Which of the following is NOT a basic element of the internal control structure for a business?

    A. Accounting procedures
    B. Independent auditor
    C. Control procedures
    D. Control environment

21. The Lighting and Design Center purchased a new floor display for a list price of $4000. Given a discount of $200, freight charges of $100, and installation costs of $150, what cost for the display will appear on the balance sheet?

    A. $3900
    B. $4000
    C. $4050
    D. $4150

22. An accountant has recorded the collection of an account receivable as a debit to cash and a credit to accounts payable. Which of the following will result if this error is not corrected?

    A. Total liabilities will be overstated
    B. Owners' equity will be overstated
    C. Total assets will be understated
    D. Total liabilities will be understated

23. The _____ depreciation method allocates an equal portion of the total depreciable cost for a plant asset to each accounting period during its useful life.

    A. declining balance
    B. units of production
    C. MACRS
    D. straight-line

24. In the last year, Blum's Nursery had sales of $695,000. The cost of goods sold was $278.000. The company's gross margin is

    A. $278,000
    B. $478,000
    C. $(478,000)
    D. $695,000

25. Bettancourt has a market value per share of $73. Its net income is $1.75 million, and the weighted-average number of shares outstanding is 350,000. Bettancourt's P/E ratio is

    A. 4.2
    B. 6.8
    C. 8.9
    D. 14.6

KEY (CORRECT ANSWERS)

1. B
2. A
3. B
4. C
5. A

6. B
7. A
8. B
9. A
10. D

11. C
12. D
13. C
14. A
15. C

16. C
17. A
18. C
19. D
20. B

21. C
22. A
23. D
24. B
25. D

TEST 3

DIRECTIONS: Each question or incomplete statement is followed by several suggested answers or completions. Select the one that BEST answers the question or completes the statement. *PRINT THE LETTER OF THE CORRECT ANSWER IN THE SPACE AT THE RIGHT.*

1. The premium on bonds payable is a(n) _____ account.

    A. adjunct liability
    B. revenue
    C. asset
    D. contra expense

2. Dividends typically appear on the

    A. statement of cash flows
    B. balance sheet
    C. income statement
    D. statement of retained earnings

3. Stoughton Manufacturing patented a new device that will not wear out for 50 years. The patent should be amortized for _____ years.

    A. 5
    B. 17
    C. 25
    D. 50

4. A 5% stock dividend

    A. decreases par value per share by 5%
    B. increases the number of shares owned by each stockholder by 5%
    C. decreases total stockholders' equity by 5%
    D. increases both the number of shares outstanding and the stockholders' equity by 5%

5. The _____ of an asset is an estimate of the amount to be recovered at the end of the asset's useful life.

    A. replacement cost
    B. book value
    C. disposal value
    D. salvage value

6. Which of the following expresses each item as a percent of the total?

    A. Income statement
    B. Common-size statement
    C. Statement of cash flows
    D. Balance sheet

7. The _____ concept of accounting is concerned with whether the failure to show an item will affect the decision-making of statement users.

   A. matching
   B. realization
   C. objectivity
   D. materiality

8. Users of financial statements are interested in determining whether the solvency and profitability of a business. For this information, they generally consult the

   A. statement of cash flows and balance sheet
   B. owners' equity statement and income statement
   C. ledger and balance sheet
   D. balance sheet and income statement

9. Johnny Corp. has an accounts receivable turnover rate of 6 and an inventory turnover rate of 8. Assuming 365 days in a year, it will take Johnny Corp about _____ days to convert its inventory to cash through normal business operations.

   A. 26
   B. 45
   C. 60
   D. 115

10. The Sterger Group signed a $30,000, noninterest-bearing, 60-day, 12% note payable at the bank. The journal entry for this transaction should include a

    A. debit to cash for $29,400
    B. debit to cash for $30,600
    C. credit to notes payable for $29,400
    D. credit to notes payable for $30,600

11. Which of the following is included in a company's cash flow from investing activities?

    A. Cash paid for employee salaries
    B. Cash paid for the purchase of capital equipment
    C. Cash received from the issue of common stock
    D. Cash paid from income taxes

12. The purchase of merchandise for resale would result in a debit to the _____ account if the periodic inventory system is used.

    A. cost of goods sold
    B. purchases
    C. merchandise inventory
    D. accounts receivable

13. An accountant is using the indirect method for the cash flow statement. In adjusting net income to arrive at net cash provided from operating activities, the accountant would

    A. add decreases in accounts payable
    B. add increases in accounts payable

C. subtract depreciation
D. add losses on equipment sales

14. Plimco sold and delivered servers to Technew for $300,000 to be paid by Technew in three equal installments over the next three months. The journal entry made by Technew to record the last of these three installments will include a debit of $100,000 to

    A. accounts payable
    B. server expense
    C. accounts receivable
    D. cash

15. The balance of a company's allowance for doubtful accounts exceeds the amount of bad debt being written off. The entry to record the write-off against the allowance account will result in

    A. a decrease in current liabilities
    B. an increase in the current period's expenses
    C. no change in the current period's expenses
    D. a decrease in current assets

16. An accountant is using the indirect method of reporting cash provided by operating activities. In this method, depreciation expense is

    A. deducted from net income
    B. added to net income
    C. netted against accumulated depreciation
    D. not included in the statement of cash flows

17. Which of the following statements about the face value of a note is FALSE?

    A. It is the value shown on the face of the note.
    B. It can represent the principal of the note.
    C. It can represent the interest earned on the note.
    D. It can be the amount borrowed on the note.

18. During the current year, the assets of The Jolly Roger increase by $73,000, and the liabilities increase by $39,000. As a result, the owners' equity

    A. is $34,000
    B. increases by $34,000
    C. decreases by $34,000
    D. decreases by $39,000

19. Which of the following would be recorded as equity?

    A. Retained earnings
    B. Merchandise inventory
    C. Land held for future plant expansion
    D. Accounts receivable

20. When preparing a bank reconciliation, deposits in transit would　　20.____

    A. decrease the book balance
    B. increase the book balance
    C. decrease the bank balance
    D. increase the bank balance

21. Stymie Corporation's retained earnings increased $40,000 during the year, and the company paid dividends of $8000. The net income or loss for the current year was　　21.____

    A. $32,000
    B. $48,000
    C. $(32,000)
    D. $(48,000)

22. Of the following, which appears in both the income statement debit column and the balance sheet credit column of a worksheet?　　22.____

    A. Retained earnings
    B. Net income
    C. Net loss
    D. Dividends

23. When the closing entry approach is used to record inventory changes, _____ merchandise inventory is _____ to remove it from the books.　　23.____

    A. beginning; credited
    B. beginning; debited
    C. ending; credited
    D. ending; debited

24. In the last year, Ling Cod Enterprises earned a gross profit of $157,500 on sales of $375,000. Its cost of goods sold was　　24.____

    A. $108,750
    B. $(217,500)
    C. $217,500
    D. $532,500

25. Each of the following is a procedure associated with a perpetual inventory system, EXCEPT　　25.____

    A. recording merchandising transactions as they occur
    B. debiting the purchase account when merchandise is acquired
    C. maintaining the inventory value after each transaction
    D. using two entries to record a sale

KEY (CORRECT ANSWERS)

1. A
2. D
3. A
4. B
5. D

6. B
7. D
8. D
9. D
10. A

11. B
12. B
13. C
14. C
15. C

16. B
17. C
18. B
19. A
20. D

21. B
22. B
23. A
24. C
25. B

TEST 4

DIRECTIONS: Each question or incomplete statement is followed by several suggested answers or completions. Select the one that BEST answers the question or completes the statement. *PRINT THE LETTER OF THE CORRECT ANSWER IN THE SPACE AT THE RIGHT.*

1. Each of the following is a major category that appears on the statement of cash flows, EXCEPT _____ activities. 1.____

   A. investment
   B. financing
   C. collecting
   D. operating

2. Fife Corporation's net income for the year was $157,250. Its average equity for the year was $850,000. What was Fife's return on equity? 2.____

   A. 1.85%
   B. 5.4%
   C. 18.5%
   D. 54%

3. What is the term for the process of transferring an amount recorded in the journal to the indicated ledger account? 3.____

   A. Transcription
   B. Footing
   C. Journalizing
   D. Posting

4. On October 5, Portis Inc. borrowed $100,000 by signing a 90-day note payable with annual interest of 9%. The amount of interest Portis will owe on this note for the month of October is 4.____

   A. $616.44
   B. $641.10
   C. $665.75
   D. $720

5. Money set aside by companies to repay bonds is known as a 5.____

   A. coupon
   B. sinking fund
   C. float
   D. debenture

6. _____ are current and past financial statements that show dollar and percent changes from previous years for each financial statement item. 6.____

   A. common-size statements
   B. comparative financial statements
   C. horizontal analyses
   D. vertical analyses

7. Which of the following is typically shown FIRST on the classified balance sheet?

   A. Current assets
   B. Long-term investments
   C. Plant assets
   D. Long-form investments

8. Graphonix purchases land and buildings, paying $125,000 in cash and offering a note payable for $75,000. This transaction will

   A. increase total assets
   B. increase owners' equity
   C. decrease total assets
   D. decrease total liability

9. An accountant is using the indirect method for the cash flow statement. In adjusting net income to arrive at net cash provided from operating activities, the accountant will add

   A. the amortization of patents
   B. increases in inventories
   C. increases in prepaid expenses
   D. gains on sales of office furniture

Questions 10 and 11 refer to the following information: On October 11, Landesman Enterprises performed services for its customers and was paid cash.

10. The October 11 journal entry would include a debit to the _____ account.

    A. liability   B. asset   C. revenue   D. expense

11. The October 11 journal entry would include a credit to the _____ account.

    A. asset
    B. liability
    C. revenue
    D. owners' equity

12. A company's net sales have increased faster than the rate of inflation, and its gross profit rate is falling. The most likely explanation for this is that

    A. there is a very strong demand for the company's products
    B. operating expenses are rising
    C. the company has lowered sales prices to achieve an increase in sales volume
    D. the company's cost of purchase merchandising is decreasing

13. The _____ principle states that revenue usually should be recognized and recorded in the accounting records when goods are sold or services rendered.

    A. cost
    B. realization
    C. going-concern
    D. time-period

14. During a period of rising prices, the _____ method of inventory valuation is likely to result in the lowest cost as ending inventory.

    A. last in, first out (LIFO)
    B. first in, first out (FIFO)
    C. weighted average
    D. gross profit

    14._____

15. When a bond sells at a premium, this means that the

    A. bond pays no interest
    B. contract rate equals the market rate
    C. contract rate is below the market rate
    D. contract rate is above the market rate

    15._____

16. A company declares and pays a cash dividend to shareholders of $20,000. Which of the following is true?

    A. Owners' equity decreases.
    B. Owners' equity increases.
    C. Owners' equity remains unchanged.
    D. Total assets increase.

    16._____

17. The price-to-book ratio of a stock is a measure of

    A. how highly the company is valued
    B. how profitable the company is
    C. the company's dividend payout
    D. how much debt is carried by a company

    17._____

18. Which of the following is a capital expenditure?

    A. Extraordinary repairs
    B. Ordinary repairs
    C. Additions
    D. Betterments

    18._____

19. Buildings used in business operations are an example of

    A. a plant asset
    B. an intangible asset
    C. current asset
    D. equity

    19._____

20. If the _____ is used, ending inventory on the balance sheet will usually be stated at current market costs

    A. specific identification method
    B. last in, first out (LIFO) cost flow assumption
    C. first in, first out, (FIFO) cost flow assumption
    D. weighted or moving average cost flow assumption

    20._____

21. Which of the following statements about available-for-sale securities is FALSE?

    A. They are not classified as trading or held-to-maturity.
    B. They are actively managed and traded.
    C. They are purchased to earn interest, dividends, or for value appreciation.
    D. They can be either debt or equity securities.

22. Which of the following is an investing activity?

    A. Reissuing treasury stock
    B. Selling land for cash
    C. Paying interest on a note payable
    D. Purchasing supplies for cash

23. The cost of all merchandise purchased for resale, including transportation in but less returns, allowances, and discounts, is expressed as

    A. cost of merchandise available for sale
    B. net cost of purchases
    C. gross cost of purchases
    D. cost of goods sold

24. The _____ method for determining an asset's depreciation expense applies a constant depreciation rate each period to the asset's beginning book value.

    A. straight-line
    B. declining balance
    C. units of production
    D. MACRS

25. Overton Timber purchased a tract of land at a cost of $1.5 million, expecting to log 2 million board-feet of lumber from the land. The salvage value of the land is expected to be $250,000. The depletion expense per board-foot of lumber is

    A. $0.625
    B. $0.75
    C. $3.25
    D. $6.00

KEY (CORRECT ANSWERS)

1.	C	11.	C
2.	C	12.	C
3.	D	13.	B
4.	B	14.	A
5.	B	15.	D
6.	C	16.	A
7.	A	17.	A
8.	A	18.	B
9.	A	19.	A
10.	B	20.	C

21. B
22. B
23. B
24. B
25. A

EXAMINATION SECTION
TEST 1

DIRECTIONS: Each question or incomplete statement is followed by several suggested answers or completions. Select the one that BEST answers the question or completes the statement. *PRINT THE LETTER OF THE CORRECT ANSWER IN THE SPACE AT THE RIGHT.*

1. The independent auditor's PRIMARY objective in reviewing internal control is to provide
   A. assurance of the client's operational efficiency
   B. a basis for reliance on the system and determination of the scope of the auditing procedures
   C. a basis for suggestions for improving the client's accounting system
   D. evidence of the client's adherence to prescribed managerial policies

   1._____

2. If there is an increase in work-in-process inventory during a period,
   A. cost of goods sold will be greater than cost of goods manufactured
   B. cost of goods manufactured will be greater than cost of goods sold
   C. manufacturing costs (production costs) for the period will be greater than cost of goods manufactured
   D. manufacturing costs for the period will be less than cost of goods manufactured

   2._____

Questions 3-4.

DIRECTIONS: Questions 3 and 4 are to be answered on the basis of the information given below about the Parr Company and the Farr Company.

The Parr Company purchased 800 of the 1,000 outstanding shares of the Farr Company's common stock for $80,000 on January 1, 2021. During 2021, the Farr Company declared dividends of $8,000 and reported earnings for the year of $20,000.

3. Using the equity method, the investment in Farr Company on the Parr Company's books should show a balance, at December 31, 2021, of
   A. $89,600 B. $$86,400 C. $80,000 D. $73,600

   3._____

4. If, instead of using the equity method, the Parr Company uses the cost method, the balance, at December 31, 2021, in the investment account, should be
   A. $96,000 B. $86,400 C. $80,000 D. $73,600

   4._____

Questions 5-6.

DIRECTIONS: Questions 5 and 6 are to be answered on the basis of the information given below about the Fame Corporation.

The Fame Corporation has 50,000 shares of $10 par value common stock authorized, issued, and outstanding. The 50,000 shares were issued at $12 per share. The retained earnings of the company are $60,000.

5. Assuming that the Fame Corporation reacquired 1,000 of its common shares at $15 per share and the par value method of accounting for treasury stock was used, the result would be that
   A. stockholders' equity would increase by $15,000
   B. capital in excess of par would decrease by at least $2,000
   C. retained earnings would decrease by $5,000
   D. common stock would decrease by at least $15,000

5.____

6. Assuming that the Fame Corporation reissued 1,000 of its common shares at $11 per share and the cost method of accounting for treasury stock was used, the result would be that
   A. book value per share of common stock would decrease
   B. retained earnings would decrease by $11,000
   C. donated surplus would be credited for $5,500
   D. a gain on reissue of treasury stock account would be charged

6.____

7. On January 31, 2012, when the Montana Corporation's stock was selling at $36 per share, its capital accounts were as follows:
   Capital Stock (par value $20; 100,000 shares issued) $2,000,000
   Premium on Capital Stock   800,000
   Retained Earnings   4,550,000
   If the corporation declares a 100% stock dividend and the par value per share remains at $20, the value of the capital stock would
   A. remain the same   B. increase to $5,600,000
   C. increase to $5,000,000   D. decrease

7.____

8. In a conventional form of the statement of sources and application of funds, which one of the following would NOT be included?
   A. Periodic amortization of premium of bonds payable
   B. Machinery, fully depreciated and scrapped
   C. Patents written off
   D. Treasury stock purchased from a stockholder

8.____

Questions 9-11.

DIRECTIONS: Questions 9 through 11 are to be answered on the basis of the balance sheet shown below for the Argo, Baron and Schooster partnership.

Cash	$ 20,000
Other assets	180,000
Total	$200,000

Liabilities	$50,000
Argo Capital (40%)	37,000
Baron Capital (40%)	65,000
Schooster Capital (20%)	48,000
Total	$200,000

9. If George is to be admitted as a new 1/6 partner without recording goodwill or bonus, George should contribute cash of
   A. $40,000   B. $36,000   C. $33,333   D. $30,000

   9.____

10. Assume that Schooster is paid $51,000 by George for his interest in the partnership.
    Which of the following choices shows the CORRECT revised capital account for each partner?
    A. Argo, $38,500; Baron, $66,500; George, $51,000
    B. Argo, $38,500; Baron, $66,500; George, $48,000
    C. Argo, $37,000; Baron, $65,000; George, $51,000
    D. Argo, $37,000; Baron, $65,000; George, $48,000

    10.____

11. Assume that George had not been admitted as a partner but that the partnership was dissolved and liquidated on the basis of the original balance sheet. Non-cash assets with a book value of $90,000 were sold for $50,000 cash. After payment of creditors, all available cash was distributed.
    Which of the following choices MOST NEARLY shows what each of the partners would receive?
    A. Argo, $0; Baron, $13,333; Schooster, $6,667
    B. Argo, $0; Baron, $3,000; Schooster, $17,000
    C. Argo, $6,667; Baron, $6,667; Schooster, $6,666
    D. Argo, $8,000; Baron, $8,000; Schooster, $4,000

    11.____

12. Which one of the following should be restricted to ONLY one employee in order to assure proper control of assets?
    A. Access to safe deposit box
    B. Placing orders and maintaining relationship with a principal vendor
    C. Collection of a particular past due account
    D. Custody of the petty cash fund

    12.____

13. To assure proper internal control, the quantities of materials ordered may be omitted from that copy of the purchase order which is
    A. sent to the accounting department
    B. retained in the purchasing department
    C. sent to the party requisitioning the material
    D. sent to the receiving department

14. The Amey Corporation has an inventory of raw materials and parts made up of many different items which are of small value individually but of significant total value
    A BASIC control requirement in such a situation is that
    A. perpetual inventory records should be maintained for all items
    B. physical inventories should be taken on a cyclical basis rather than at year end
    C. storekeeping, production, and inventory record-keeping functions should be separated
    D. requisitions for materials should be approved by a corporate officer

15. In conducting an audit of plant assets, which of the following accounts MUST be examined in order to ascertain that additions to plant assets have been correctly stated and reflect charges that are properly capitalized?
    A. Accounts Receivable
    B. Sales Income
    C. Maintenance and Repairs
    D. Investments

16. Which one of the following is a control procedure that would prevent a vendor's invoice from being paid twice (once upon the original invoice and once upon the monthly statement?
    A. Attaching the receiving report to the disbursement support papers
    B. Prenumbering of disbursement vouchers
    C. Using a limit of reasonable test
    D. Prenumbering of receiving reports

17. A "cut-off" bank statement is received for the period December 1 to December 10, 2021. Very few of the checks listed on the November 30, 2021 bank reconciliation cleared during the cut-off period.
    Of the following, the MOST likely reason for this is
    A. kiting
    B. using certified checks rather than ordinary checks
    C. holding the cash disbursement book open after year end
    D. overstating year-end bank balance

18. "Lapping" is a common type of defalcation.
    Of the audit techniques listed below, the one MOST effective in the detection of "lapping" is
    A. reconciliation of year-end bank statements
    B. review of duplicate deposit slips
    C. securing confirmations from banks
    D. checking footings in cash journals

19. Of the following, the MOST common argument against the use of the negative accounts receivable confirmation is that
    A. cost per response is excessively high
    B. statistical sampling techniques cannot be applied to selection of the sample
    C. client's customers may assume that the confirmation is a request for payment
    D. lack of response does not necessarily indicate agreement with the balance

Questions 20-21.

DIRECTIONS   Questions 20 and 21 are to be answered on the basis of the information in the Payroll Summary given below. This Payroll Summary represents payroll for a monthly period for a particular agency.

		PAYROLL SUMMARY				
		Deductions				
Employee	Total Earnings	FICA	Withhold Tax	State Tax	Other	Net Pay
W	450.00	26.00	67.00	18.00	6.00	333.00
X	235.00	14.00	33.00	8.00	2.00	178.00
Y	341.00	20.00	52.00	14.00	5.00	250.00
Z	275.00	16.00	30.00	6.00	2.40	220.60
Totals	1,301.00	76.00	182.00	46.00	15.40	981.60

20. Based on the data given above, the amount of cash that would have to be available to pay the employees on payday is
    A. $1,301.00   B. $981.60   C. $905.60   D. $662.60

21. Based on the data given above, the amount of cash that would have to be governmental depository is
    A. $334.00   B. $182.00   C. $158.00   D. $76.00

Questions 22-23.

DIRECTIONS: Questions 22 and 23 are to be answered on the basis of the information given below concerning an imprest fund.

Assume a $1,020 imprest fund for cash expenditures is maintained in your agency. As an audit procedure, the fund is counted and the following information results from that count.

Unreimbursed bills properly authorized	$ 345.00
Check from employee T. Jones	125.00
Check from Supervisor R. Riggles	250.00
I.O.U. signed by employee J. Sloan	100.00
Cash counted—coins and bills	200.00
TOTAL	$1,020.00

22. A PROPER statement of cash on hand based upon the data shown above should show a balance of 22.____
   A. $1,020   B. $1,000   C. $545   D. $200

23. Based upon the data shown above, the account reflects IMPROPER handling of the fund because 23.____
   A. vouchers are unreimbursed
   B. the cash balance is too low
   C. employees have used it for loans and check-cashing purposes
   D. the unreimbursed bills should not have been authorized

Question 24-25.

DIRECTIONS: Questions 24 and 25 are to be answered on the basis of the following information.

The following information was taken from the ledgers of the Past Present Corporation:

Common stock had been issued for $6,000,000. This represents 400,000 shares of stock at a stated value of $5 per share. Fifty-thousand shares are in the treasury. These 50,000 shares were acquired for $25 per share. The total undistributed net income since the origin of the corporation was $3,750,000 as of December 31, 2021. Ten-thousand of the treasury stock shares were sold in January 2022 for $30 per share.

24. Based only on the information given above, the TOTAL stockholders' equity that should have been shown on the balance sheet as of December 31, 2021 was 24.____
   A. $2,000,000   B. $6,000,000   C. $8,500,000   D. $9,750,000

25. Based only on the information given above, the Retained Earnings as of December 31, 2022 will be 25.____
   A. $2,000,000   B. $3,750,000   C. $3,800,000   D. $4,050,000

Questions 26-29.

DIRECTIONS: Questions 26 through 29 are to be answered on the basis of the following information.

A statement of income for the Dartmouth Corporation for the 2022 fiscal year follows:

Sales	$89,000	
Cost of Goods Sold	20,000	
Gross Margin		$34,000
Expenses		20,000
Net Income Before Income Taxes		$14,000
Provision for Income Taxes (50%)		7,000
Net Income		$7,000

The following errors were discovered relating to the 2022 fiscal year:
- Closing inventory was overstated by $2,100
- A $3,000 expenditure was capitalized during fiscal year 2022 that should have been listed under Expenses. This was subject to 10% amortization taken for a full year
- Sales included $3,500 of deposits received from customers for future orders.
- Accrued salaries of $850 were not included in Cost of Goods Sold
- Interest receivable of $500 was omitted

Assume that the books were not closed and that you have prepared a corrected income statement. Answer Questions 26 through 29 on the basis of your corrected income statement.

26. The gross margin after accounting for adjustments SHOULD BE
    A. $37,500   B. $35,400   C. $31,900   D. $27,550

27. The adjusted income before income taxes SHOULD BE
    A. $5,350   B. $9,550   C. $15,000   D. $15,850

28. The adjusted income after provision for a 50% tax rate SHOULD BE
    A. $7,925   B. $7,500   C. $4,500   D. $2,675

29. After making adjustments, sales to be reported for fiscal year 2022 SHOULD BE
    A. unchanged
    B. increased by $3,500
    C. decreased by $3,500
    D. reduced by $2,100

Questions 30-33.

DIRECTIONS: Questions 30 through 33 are to be answered on the basis of the following budget for the Utility Corporation for 2022.

Sales	$550,000
Cost of Goods Sold	320,000
Selling Expenses	75,000
General Expenses	60,000
Net Income	95,000

30. If sales are actually 12% above the budget, then ACTUAL sales will be
    A. $550,000   B. $562,000   C. $605,000   D. $616,000

31. If actual costs of goods sold exceed the budget by 10%, then the cost of goods sold will be
    A. $294,400   B. $320,000   C. $605,000   D. $352,000

32. If selling expenses exceed the budget by 10%, the INCREASE in the selling expenses will be
    A. $750   B. $3,750   C. $7,500   D. $8,333

8 (#1)

33. If general expenses are under budget by 5%, they will amount to 33.____
  A. $3,000   B. $57,000   C. $60,000   D. $63,000

Questions 34-35.

DIRECTIONS: Questions 34 and 35 are to be answered on the basis of the following information.

The Yontiff Company began business on January 2, 2021. During the first month, credit sales totaled $100,000. During February, credit sales totaled $125,000. 70% of credit sales are paid during the month of sale, and the balance is collected during the following month.

34. During the month of January, cash collections on credit sales totaled 34.____
  A. $70,000   B. $95,000   C. $100,000   D. $125,000

35. During the month of February, cash collections on credit sales totaled 35.____
  A. $70,000   B. $87,500   C. $117,505   D. $125,000

Questions 36-38.

DIRECTIONS: Questions 36 through 38 are to be answered on the basis of the following information taken from the balance sheet of the F Corporation.

  Common Stock $200 Par $1,400,000
  Premium on Common Stock   115,000
  Deficit   50,000

36. The number of shares of common stock outstanding is 36.____
  A. 200   B. 700   C. 7,000   D. 14,000

37. The total equity is 37.____
  A. $50,000   B. $115,000   C. $1,400,000   D. $1,465,000

38. The book value per share of stock is MOST NEARLY 38.____
  A. $160   B. $200   C. $209   D. $312

Questions 39-40.

DIRECTIONS: Questions 39 and 40 are to be answered on the basis of the following statement.

You are examining the expense accounts of a contractor and you discover that, although his payroll records show proper deductions from employees, he has never provided for the payroll tax expenses for these employees.

39. As a result of the oversight described in the above statement, the Costs of 39.____
  Construction in Progress as given on the balance sheet will be _____ on the balance sheet.
  A. understated   B. overstated   C. unaffected   D. omitted

40. As a result of the oversight described in the above statement, the balance sheet for the firm will reflect an
    A. overstatement of liabilities
    B. understatement of liabilities
    C. overstatement of assets
    D. understatement of assets

40._____

KEY (CORRECT ANSWERS)

1.	B	11.	D	21.	A	31.	D
2.	C	12.	D	22.	D	32.	C
3.	A	13.	D	23.	C	33.	B
4.	C	14.	C	24.	C	34.	A
5.	B	15.	C	25.	B	35.	C
6.	A	16.	A	26.	D	36.	C
7.	A	17.	C	27.	A	37.	D
8.	B	18.	B	28.	D	38.	C
9.	D	19.	D	29.	C	39.	A
10.	D	20.	B	30.	D	40.	B

TEST 2

DIRECTIONS: Each question or incomplete statement is followed by several suggested answers or completions. Select the one that BEST answers the question or completes the statement. *PRINT THE LETTER OF THE CORRECT ANSWER IN THE SPACE AT THE RIGHT.*

Questions 1-4.

DIRECTIONS: Questions 1 through 4 are to be answered on the basis of the following information.

In the audit of the Audell Co. for the calendar year 2021, the accountant noted the following errors.

- An adjusting entry for $10 for interest accrued on a customer's $4,000, 60-day, 6% note was not recorded at the end of December 2020. In 2021, the total interest received was credited to interest income.
- Equipment was leased on December 31, 2020 and rental of $300 was paid in advance for the next three months and charged to Rent Expense.
- On November 1, 2020, space was rented at $75 per month. The tenant paid six months rent in advance which was credited to Rent Income.
- Salary expenses in the amount of $60 were not recorded at the end of 2020
- Depreciation in the amount of $80 was not recorded at the end of 2020.
- An error of $200 in addition on the year-end 2020 physical inventory sheets was made. The inventory was overstated.

1. The amount of the net adjustment to Net Income for 2020 is
   A. Credit $430   B. Debit $430   C. Credit $600   D. Credit $560

2. The net change in asset values at December 31, 2020 is
   A. Credit $70   B. Debit $70   C. Debit $110   D. Credit $60

3. The net change in liabilities at December 31, 2020 is
   A. Debit $360   B. Credit $430   C. Debit $560   D. Credit $360

4. The net change in Owner's Equity at December 31, 2020 is   4.____
   A. Debit $720   B. Debit $430   C. Credit $320   D. Credit $720

5. As of October 2, 2021, the Mallory Company's books reflect a balance of $2,104.75 in its account entitled Cash in Bank. A comparison of the book entries with the bank statement showed the following:
   - A check in the amount of $76.25 outstanding at the end of September 2021 had not been returned.
   - One check, which was returned with the October bank statement, in the amount of $247 had been recorded in the October cash book as $274.
   - A total of $139 of checks issued in October had not been returned with the October bank statement.
   - A deposit of $65 was returned by the bank because of insufficient funds.

- The bank charged a service charge of $3.25 for the month of October which as not reported on the books until November.
- The bank had credited $247 representing a note collected in the amount of $250 which was not picked up on the books until November.
- A deposit of $305.50 was recorded on the books in October but not on the bank statement.

The balance in the bank as shown on the bank statement at October 31, 2021 is
  A. $2,220.25   B. $2,104.75   C. $2,006.25   D. $2,315.25

Questions 6-8.

DIRECTIONS: Questions 6 through 8 are to be answered on the basis of the following information.

A company purchased three cars at $3,150 each on April 2, 2021. Depreciation is to be computed on a mileage basis. The estimated mileage to be considered is 50,000 miles, with a trade-in value of $650 for each car.

After having been driven 8,400 miles, car #1 was completely destroyed on November 23, 2020 and not replaced. The insurance company paid $2,500 for the loss.

As of December 31, 2020, of the two remaining cars, car #2 had been driven 10,300 miles and car #3 was driven 11,500 miles.

On July 10, 2021, after having been driven a total of 24,600 miles, car #2 was sold for $1,800.

Car #3, after having been driven a total of 27,800 miles, was traded in on December 28, 2021 for a new car (#4) that had a list price of $3,000. On the purchase of car #4, the dealer allowed a trade-in value of $1,850.

6. The balance in the Allowance for Depreciation account at December 31, 2020 is   6.____
    A. $1,850   B. $910   C. $1,090   D. $1,110

7. The depreciation expense for the calendar year 2021 is   7.____
    A. $1,530   B. $2,000   C. $2,500   D. $3,00

8. The book value of the new car (car #4) using the income tax method is   8.____
    A. $1,850   B. $3,000   C. $2,500   D. $2,910

Questions 9-10.

DIRECTIONS: Questions 9 and 10 are to be answered on the basis of the following information.

The Pneumatic Corp. showed the following balance sheets at December 31, 2020 and December 31, 2021

	12/31/2020	12/31/2021
Cash	$6,700	$9,000
Accounts Receivable	12,000	11,500
Merchandise Inventory	31,500	32,000
Prepaid Expenses	800	1,000
Equipment	21,000	28,000
	$72,000	$81,500
Accumulated Depreciation	$4,000	$5,500
Accounts Payable	17,500	11,500
Common Stock - $5 Per Share	10,000	5,000
Premium on Common Stock	40,000	50,000
Retained Earnings	10,500	13,000
	$72,000	$81,500

Additional Information:
A further examination of the Pneumatic Corp.'s transactions for 2021 showed the following:
- Depreciation on equipment, $2,500]
- Fully depreciated equipment that cost $1,000 was scrapped, and cost and related accumulated depreciation eliminated.
- Two thousand shares of common stock were sold at $6 per share.
- A cash dividend of $10,000 was paid.

9. A statement of funds provided and applied for the calendar year 2021 would show that net income provided funds in the amount of
    A. $2,500   B. $9,500   C. $15,000   D. $22,500

10. The funds applied to the acquisition of equipment during the calendar year 2021 amounts to
    A. $21,000   B. $28,000   C. $1,000   D. $8,000

11. A company's Wage Expense account had a $19,100 debit balance before any adjustment at the end of its December 31, 2020 fiscal year. The company employs five individuals who earn $15 per day and were paid on Friday for the five days ending on Friday, December 25, 2020. All employees worked during the week ending January 2, 2021.
    The adjusted balance in the Wage Expense account at December 31, 2020 is
    A. $22,300   B. $19,100   C. $19,250   D. $19,325

Questions 12-13.

DIRECTIONS: Questions 12 and 13 are to be answered on the basis of the following information.

4 (#2)

The Peach Corp.'s books reflect an account entitled "Allowance for Bad Debts" showing a credit balance of $1,510 as of January 1, 2020.

During 2020, it wrote off 735 of bad debts and increased the allowance for bad debts by an amount equal to ¼ of 1% of sales of $408,000.

During 2021, it wrote off $605 as bad debts and recorded $50 of a debt that had been previously written off.

An addition to the "Allowance for Bad Debts" was provided based upon ¼ of 1% on $478,000 of sales.

12. The balance in the "Allowance for Bad Debts" account at December 31, 2021 is   12.____
    A. $2,550   B. $2,434   C. $2,360   D. $2,240

13. The amount of the Bad Debt expense for the calendar year 2021 is   13.____
    A. $1,195   B. $1,405   C. $2,000   D. $1,510

14. The following ratio is based upon the 2021 financial statements of the Chino Corp.:   14.____
Number of Times Bond Interest Earned: $28,000/$3,000 = 9.33 times
Information relating to the corrections of the income data for 2021 follows:
- Rental payment for December 2021 at $2,00 per month had been recorded in January 2022. No provision has been made for this expense on the 2021 books.
- During 2021, merchandise shipped on consignment and unsold had been recorded as
    Debit – Accounts Receivable $4,000
    Credit – Sales   4,000

(Note: The inventory of this merchandise was properly recorded.)
If the described ratio, Number of Times Bond Interest Earned, was recomputed, taking into consideration the corrections listed above and ignoring tax factors in the calculations, the recomputed <u>Number of Times Bond Interest Earned</u> would be _____ times.
    A. 8.10   B. 7.60   C. 6.20   D. 5.10

Questions 15-16.

DIRECTIONS: Questions 15 and 16 are to be answered on the basis of the following information.

The Delancey Department Store, Inc. sells merchandise on the installment basis. The selling price of its merchandise is $500 and its cost is $325.

At the end of its fiscal year, an examination of its accounts showed the following:
    Sales (Installment $500,000
    Installment Accounts Receivable   280,000
    Sales Commissions   15,000
    Other Expenses   32,000

15. The net income for the fiscal year, before taxes, using the installment method   15.____
    of reporting income, is
    A. $30,000   B. $20,000   C. $15,000   D. $35,000

16. The balance in the Deferred Income Account at the end of the fiscal year is   16.____
    A. $110,000   B. $80,000   C. $76,000   D. $98,000

Questions 17-18.

DIRECTIONS: Questions 17 and 18 are to be answered on the basis of the following information.

The Merrimac Company sold 8,800 units of a product at $5 per unit during the calendar year 2021. In addition, it has the following transactions:

	Units	Unit Cost
Inventory – January 1, 2021	1,000	$2.80
Purchases – March	1,000	3.00
June	4,000	3.20
September	3,000	3.30
October	1,000	3.50

17. If we assume that selling and administrative expenses cost $8,800, the Net   17.____
    Income for the calendar year 2021, using the first-in first-out method of costing
    inventory is
    A. $8,460   B. $7,360   C. $6,600   D. $4,070

18. If we assume that selling and administrative expenses cost $8,800, the Net   18.____
    Income for the calendar year 2021, using the last-in first-out method of costing
    inventory, is
    A. $4,550   B. $7,360   C. $6,600   D. $5,000

19. L. Eron and A. Pilott are partners who share income and losses in the ratio   19.____
    3:2, respectively. The balance in the Profit and Loss account on December 31,
    2021, prior to distribution to the partners, is $20,800. Before distributing any
    profits to the partnership in the agreed ratio, L. Eron is to be given credit for
    interest on his loan of $60,000, outstanding for the entire year, at 6% per
    annum. A. Pilott is to receive a bonus of 10% of the net income over $5,100,
    after deducting the bonus to himself and the interest to L. Eron.
    Giving consideration to all the above information, the total amount of net
    income to be credited to A. Pilott is
    A. $8,320   B. $2,080   C. $7,540   D. $15,700

Questions 20-21.

DIRECTIONS: Questions 20 and 21 are to be answered on the basis of the following information.

Schneider and Samuels are partners with capital balances on December 31, 2021 of $15,000 and $25,000, respectively. They share profits in a ratio of 2:1.

Goroff is to be admitted to the partnership. He agrees to be admitted as a partner with a cash investment to give him a one-third interest in the capital and profits of the business. All the parties agree that the goodwill to be granted to Goroff should be valued at $6,000.

20. The required cash to cover Goroff's investment in a business partnership according to the terms stated is 20.____
 A. $20,000 B. $14,000 C. $6,000 D. $25,000

21. After his cash investment, and all other initial entries, the credit to Goroff's Capital account is 21.____
 A. $20,000 B. $14,000 C. $6,000 D. $25,000

22. The Marlin Corp. sold 7,800 units of its product at $25 per unit and suffered a net loss for its calendar year ending December 31, 2021 of $2,000. The fixed expenses amounted to $80,000 and the variable expenses $117,000. The Marlin Corp. believes that by expending $20,000 in an advertising campaign, it could increase its sales, retaining the $25 per unit selling price, to generate a profit. 22.____
 Assuming the above facts, the sales revenue for 2021 reflecting the break-even point is
 A. $195,000 B. $217,000 C. $250,000 D. $300,000

23. The Anide Corp., which keeps its books on the accrual basis, had the following transactions for its calendar year ending December 31, 2021. 23.____
 - April 15, 2021 – Authorized the issuance of $3,000,000 of 5.5%, 20 year bonds, dated May 1, 2021. Interest to be paid November 1 and May 1.
 - June 1, 2021 – Sold the entire issue at $2,965,150 plus accrued interest
 - November 1, 2021 – Paid the interest due.
 The interest expense for the calendar year 2021 is
 A. $85,000 B. $165,000 C. $110,000 D. $97,300

Questions 24-26.

DIRECTIONS: Questions 24 through 26 are to be answered on the basis of the following information.

The following information was taken from a worksheet that was used in the preparation of the balance sheet and the profit and loss statement of the Hott Company for 2021.

The Balance Sheet Contained	Amount
Travel Expense Unpaid	$995
Legal and Collection Fees – Prepaid in Advance	672
Interest Received in Advance	469

The Profit and Loss Statement Contained	Amount
Travel Expenses	$7,343
Legal and Collection Fees	5,461
Interest Income	3,114

The proper adjusting and closing entries were made on the books of the company by the accountant and the described information was reported on the financial statements. The books are kept on an accrual basis.

On the basis of the above facts, the balance in each of the following accounts in the trial balance, before adjusting and closing entries were made, was as follows:

24. Travel Expense Account
    A. $8,338   B. $7,343   C. $6,348   D. $995

25. Legal and Collection Fees Account
    A. $672   B. $4,789   C. $5,461   D. $6,133

26. Interest Income Account
    A. $3,583   B. $3,114   C. $2,645   D. $469

Questions 27-28.

DIRECTIONS: Questions 27 and 28 are to be answered on the basis of the following information

The following is the stockholder's equity section of a corporation:
Preferred Stock (7%, cumulative, non-participating, $100 par value
, 5,000 shares issued and outstanding) $500.000

Common Stock ($1.00 par value, 500,000, issued and outstanding)   500,000
                                                                                              $1,000,000

Deficit   (40,000)
                                                                                                 $960,000

27. Assuming two years' dividends in arrears on the preferred stock, the book value per share of common stock is
    A. 78¢   B. 80¢   C. 63¢   D. 94¢

28. Assuming two years' dividends in arrears on the preferred stock, the book value per share of preferred stock is
    A. $130   B. $114   C. $98   D. $140

Questions 29-30.

DIRECTIONS: Questions 29 and 30 are to be answered on the basis of the following information.

Regina Corporation on December 31, 2021 had the following stockholder's equity:

Common Stock ($10 par value), 10,000 shares authorized and outstanding)	$100,000
Retained Earnings	20,000
	$120,000

On December 31, 2021, the Astro Corp. purchased 9,000 shares of the Regina Corporation's outstanding shares, paying $14 per share

29. The entry to eliminate Astro Corp.'s investment and the Regina Corporation's stockholder's equity on consolidation would show a debit or credit to an account called "Excess of Cost Over Book Value" of
    A. Credit, $18,000
    B. Debit, $18,000
    C. Debit, $15,000
    D. Debit, $19,000

30. If the Regina Corporation had earnings for the calendar year 2021 of $10,000 and had paid out $8,000 of these earnings as dividends, and an entry to eliminate the Astro Corp.'s investment and the Regina Corporation's stockholder's equity were made, the minority stockholder's equity would be
    A. $15,000   B. $10,100   C. $12,200   D. $14,800

KEY (CORRECT ANSWERS)

1.	B	11.	D	21.	A
2.	A	12.	B	22.	C
3.	D	13.	A	23.	D
4.	B	14.	B	24.	C
5.	A	15.	A	25.	D
6.	C	16.	D	26.	A
7.	A	17.	B	27.	A
8.	D	18.	C	28.	B
9.	C	19.	C	29.	B
10.	D	20.	B	30.	C

TEST 3

DIRECTIONS: Each question or incomplete statement is followed by several suggested answers or completions. Select the one that BEST answers the question or completes the statement. *PRINT THE LETTER OF THE CORRECT ANSWER IN THE SPACE AT THE RIGHT.*

1. For the measurement of net income to be as realistic as possible, it is DESIRABLE that revenue be recognized at the point that
   A. cash is collected from customers
   B. an order for merchandise or services is received from a customer
   C. a deposit or advance payment is received from a customer
   D. goods are delivered or services are rendered to customers

   1.____

2. An accounting principle must receive substantial authoritative support to qualify as "generally accepted."
   Many organizations and agencies have been influential in the development of generally accepted accounting principles, but the MOST influential leadership has come from the
   A. New York Stock Exchange
   B. American Institute of Certified Public Accountants
   C. Securities and Exchange Commission
   D. American Accounting Association

   2.____

3. In which one of the following ways does the declaration and payment of a cash dividend affect corporate net income? It _____ net income.
   A. does not affect   B. reduces
   C. increases   D. capitalizes

   3.____

4. Under which one of the following headings of the corporate balance sheet should the liability for a dividend payable in stock appear?
   A. Current Liabilities   B. Long Term Liabilities
   C. Stockholders' Equity   D. Current Assets

   4.____

5. In which one of the following is "Working Capital" MOST likely to be found?
   A. Income Statement
   B. Analysis of Retained Earnings
   C. Computation of Cost of Capital
   D. Statement of Funds Provided and Applied

   5.____

6. Which one of the following procedures is NOT generally mandatory in auditing a merchandising corporation?
   A. Physical observation of inventory count
   B. Written circularization of accounts receivable
   C. Confirmation of bank balance
   D. Circularization of the stockholders

   6.____

7. A company purchased office supplies during 2021 in the total amount of $1,400 and charged the entire amount to the asset account. An inventory of supplies taken on December 31, 2021 shows the cost of unused supplies to be $250. The entry to record this fact, assuming the books have not been closed, involves
    A. credit to capital
    B. debit to supplies Expense
    C. credit to supplies expense
    D. debit to supplies on hand

7.____

8. A corporation's records show $600,000 (credit) in net sales, $200,000 (debit) in year-end accounts receivable, and $2,000 (debit) in Allowance for Bad Debts. The company's aged schedule of accounts receivable indicates a probable future loss from failure to collect year-end receivables in the amount of $6,000.
Of the following, the MOST correct entry to adjust the Allowance for Bad Debts at year-end is
    A. $1,000 credit
    B. $4,000 credit
    C. $8,000 debit
    D. $8,000 credit

8.____

Questions 9-10.

DIRECTIONS: Questions 9 and 10 are to be answered on the basis of the following information.

A company commenced business in 2021 and purchased inventory as follows:

March	100 units @	$5	$500
June	300	6	1,800
October	200	7	1,400
November	500	6	3,500
December	100	6	600
TOTAL	1,200		$7,800

**Units sold in 2021 amounted to 1,200

9. Under the LIFO inventory principle, the value of the remaining inventory is
    A. $1,700   B. $1,875   C. $2,145   D. $2,225

9.____

10. Under the FIFO inventory principle, the value of the remaining inventory is
    A. $1,650   B. $1,875   C. $2,000   D. $2,025

10.____

11. When doing a trial balance, assume that, as a result of a single error, the total of the credit balances is greater than the total of the debit balances. Which one of the following single errors could NOT be the cause of this discrepancy?
    A. Failure to post a debit
    B. Posting a debit as a credit
    C. Failure to post a credit
    D. Posting a credit twice

11.____

Questions 12-13.

DIRECTIONS: Questions 12 and 13 are to be answered on the basis of the following information.

A and B are partners with capital balances of $20,000 and $30,000, respectively, at June 30, 2021, who share profits and losses, 40% and 60%, respectively. On July 1, 2021, C is to be admitted into the partnership under the following conditions:
- Partnership assets are to be revalued and increased by $10,000
- C is to invest $40,000 but be credited for $30,000 while the remaining $10,000 is to be credited to A and B to compensate them for their pre-existing goodwill.

12. After C is admitted and the proper entries are made, A's capital account will have a credit balance of
    A. $24,500   B. $28,000   C. $30,200   D. $36,000

13. After the admission of C to the partnership, C's share of profits and losses is agreed upon at 20%.
    Assuming no other adjustments, the new percentage for profit and loss distribution to A will be
    A. 18%   B. 32%   C. 36%   D. 45%

14. A company reports as income for tax purposes $70,000 and its book income before the provision for income taxes is $100,000.
    Assuming a 50% tax rate, the PROPER tax expense to be recorded following tax allocation procedures is
    A. $33,000   B. $40,000   C. $50,000   D. $60,000

15. The relationship between the total of cash and current receivables to total current liabilities is commonly referred to by accountants as the
    A. acid-test ratio   B. cross-statement ratio
    C. current ratio   D. R.O.I. ratio

16. On a statement of sources and application of funds, the depreciation expense is normally shown as a(n)
    A. addition to operating income   B. subtraction from funds provided
    C. addition to funds applied   D. reduction from operating income

17. Company A owns 100% of the capital stock of Company B and reports on a consolidated basis. During the year, Company A sold inventory to Company B at a profit of $100,000. One-half of this inventory has been sold at year-end by Company B to the public.
    Which one of the following would be the MOST correct adjustment, if any, to make the consolidated retained earnings conform to generally accepted accounting principles?
    A. Decrease by $50,000   B. Increase by $50,000
    C. Increase by $100,000   D. No adjustment

4 (#3)

18. X, Y, and Z are partners with capital of $11,000, $12,000, and $4,500. X has a loan due from the partnership to him of $2,000. Profits and losses are shared in the ratio of 4:5:1, respectively. The partnership has paid off all outside liabilities, and its remaining assets consist of $9,000 in cash and $20,500 of accounts receivable. The partners agree to disburse the $9,000 to themselves in such a way that, even if one of the receivables is realized, no partner will have been overpaid.
Under these conditions, which of the following MOST NEARLY represents the amount to be paid to partner X?
   A. $1,960   B. $3,200   C. $4,800   D. $5,000

18.____

19. R Company needs $2,000,000 to finance an expansion of plant facilities. The company expects to earn a return of 15% on this investment before considering the cost of capital or income taxes. The average income tax rate for the R Company is 40%.
If the company raises the funds by issuing 6% bonds at face value, the earnings available to common stockholders after the new plant facilities are in operation may be expected to increase by
   A. $65,000   B. $70,000   C. $108,000   D. $116,000

19.____

20. The budget for a given factory overhead cost was $150,000 for the year. The actual cost for the year was $125,000.
Based on these facts, it can be said that the plant manager has done a better job than expected in controlling this cost if the cost is a
   A. semi-variable cost
   B. variable cost and actual production was 83 1/3% of budgeted production
   C. semi-variable cost which includes a fixed element of $25,000 per period
   D. variable cost and actual production was equal to budgeted production

20.____

21. The Home Office account on the books of the City Branch shows a credit balance of $15,000 at the end of a year and the City Branch account on the books of the Home Office shows a debit balance of $12,000.
Of the following, the MOST likely reason for the discrepancy in the two accounts is that
   A. merchandise shipped by the Home Office to the branch has not been recorded by the branch
   B. the Home Office has not recorded a branch loss for the first quarter of the year
   C. the branch has just mailed a check for $3,000 to the Home Office which has not yet been received by the Home Office
   D. the Home Office has not yet recorded the branch profit for the first quarter of the year

21.____

22. The concept of matching costs and revenues means that
   A. the expenses offset against revenues should be related to the same time period
   B. revenues are at least as great as expenses on the average
   C. revenues and expenses are equal
   D. net income equals revenues minus expenses for the same earning period

22.____

23. If the inventory at the end of the current year is understated, and the error is not caught during the following year, the effect is to
    A. *overstate* the income for the two-year period
    B. *overstate* income this year and *understate* income next year
    C. *understate* income this year and *overstate* income next year
    D. *understate* income this year, with no effect on the income of the next year

23._____

KEY (CORRECT ANSWERS)

1.	D		11.	C
2.	B		12.	B
3.	A		13.	B
4.	C		14.	C
5.	D		15.	A
6.	D		16.	A
7.	B		17.	A
8.	D		18.	C
9.	A		19.	C
10.	C		20.	D

21. D
22. A
23. C

ACCOUNTING

EXAMINATION SECTION
TEST 1

DIRECTIONS: Each question or incomplete statement is followed by several suggested answers or completions. Select the one that *BEST* answers the question or completes the statement. *PRINT THE LETTER OF THE CORRECT ANSWER IN THE SPACE AT THE RIGHT.*

Questions 1-5.

DIRECTIONS: Assume that you are requested to verify certain financial data with respect to the various business entities described below. This information is required to verify that tax returns and/or other financial reports submitted to your agency are correct.

In an auditing review of the income statements of several business firms (Companies X, Y, and Z), you find the financial information given below. Based upon the account balances shown, select the correct answer for the statement information requested.

<u>Company X</u> -
Sales $ 160,000
Opening Inventory $ 70,000
Purchases $ 80,000
Purchase Returns $ 1,200
Cost of Goods Sold $ 127,000

1. The ending inventory based upon the data above is

    A. $21,800   B. $23,000   C. $24,200   D. $33,000

<u>Company Y</u> -
Opening Inventory $ 50,000
Purchases $ 145,000
Ending Inventory $ 28,500
Gross Profit $ 56,000
Sales and Administrative Expenses $ 64,000

2. Sales for the period based upon the data above are

    A. $110,500   B. $166,500   C. $222,500   D. $286,500

<u>Company Z</u> -
Sales for the period $ 200,000
Net Profit   7% of Sales
Purchases $ 180,000
Ending Inventory $ 70,000
Gross Profit $ 60,000

3. Cost of Goods sold for Company Z is

    A. $110,000   B. $140,000   C. $180,000   D. $250,000

4. The opening inventory of Company Z would be

    A. $10,000   B. $20,000   C. $30,000   D. $80,000

5. The operating expenses for Company Z would be

    A. $10,000   B. $14,000   C. $20,000   D. $46,000

Questions 6-8.

DIRECTIONS: The following information is taken from the books and records of a business firm:

Sales for the calendar year 2018:	$52,000
Based upon FIFO Inventory:	
Good available for Sale	$46,900
Inventory at December 31, 2018	$12,700
Based upon LIFO Inventory:	
Goods available for Sale	$46,900
Inventory at December 31, 2018	$10,400

6. If FIFO Inventory valuation is used, the Gross Profit will be

   A. $5,100   B. $15,500   C. $17,800   D. $34,200

7. If LIFO Inventory valuation method is used, the Gross Profit will be

   A. $2,300   B. $15,500   C. $17,800   D. $36,500

8. If LIFO Inventory method is used, compared with the FIFO method, the cost of goods sold will be

   A. more by $2,300   B. less by $2,300
   C. more by $10,400   D. less by $12,700

9. Which one of the following would NOT properly be classified as an asset on the balance sheet of a business firm?

   A. Investment in stock of another firm
   B. Premium cost of a three-year fire insurance policy
   C. Cash surrender value of life insurance on life of corporate officer. Policy is owned by the company and the company is the beneficiary
   D. Amounts owing to employees for services rendered

10. Which one of the following would NOT properly be classified as a current asset?

   A. Travel advances to salespeople
   B. Postage in a postage meter
   C. Cash surrender value of life insurance policy on an officer, which policy names the corporation as the beneficiary
   D. Installment notes receivable due over 18 months in accordance with normal trade practice

11. Able, Baker and Carr formed a partnership. Able contributed $10,000, Baker contributed $5,000, and Carr contributed an automobile with a fair market value of $5,000. They have no partnership agreement. The first year the partnership earned $18,000. The partners will share the profits as follows:

   A. Able, $9,000; Baker, $4,500; Carr, $4,500
   B. Able, $6,000; Baker, $6,000; Carr, $6,000
   C. Able, $12,000; Baker, $6,000; Carr, No share
   D. Able, $8,000; Baker, $5,000; Carr, $5,000

Questions 12-13.

DIRECTIONS: Answer Questions 12 through 13 based on the information below.

The XYZ partnership had the following balance sheet as of December 31, 2018.

Cash	$ 5,000	Liabilities	$12,000
Other assets	40,000	X Capital	20,000
Total	$45,000	Y Capital	10,000
		Z Capital	3,000
		Total	$45,000

The partners shared profits equally. They decided to liquidate the partnership at December 31, 2018.

12. If the other assets were sold for $52,000, each partner will be entitled to a final cash distribution of

   A. X, $15,000; Y, $15,000; Z, $15,000
   B. X, $24,000; Y, $14,000; Z, $ 7,000
   C. X, $20,000; Y, $10,000; Z, $ 3,000
   D. X, $23,000; Y, $13,000; Z, $ 6,000

12.____

13. If the other assets were sold for $31,000, each partner will be entitled to a final cash distribution of

   A. X, $14,000; Y, $ 5,000; Z, $5,000
   B. X, $ 8,000; Y, R 8,000; Z, $8,000
   C. X, $15,000; Y, $15,000; Z, $15,000
   D. X, $17,000; Y, $ 7,000; Z, No cash share

13.____

14. Items selling for $40 for which there were 10% selling costs were purchased for inventory at $20 each. Selling prices and costs remained steady but at the date of the financial statement the market price had dropped to $16. The inventory remaining from the original purchase was written down to $16.
Of the following, it is correct to state that the

   A. cost of sales of the subsequent year will be overstated
   B. current year's income is overstated
   C. income of the following year will be overstated
   D. closing inventory of the current year is overstated

14.____

15. Dividends in arrears on a cumulative preferred stock should be reported on the balance sheet as

   A. an accrued liability
   B. restricted retained earnings
   C. an explanatory note
   D. a deduction from preferred stock

15.____

16. The effect of recording the payment of a 10% dividend paid in stock would be to

   A. increase the current ratio
   B. decrease the amount of working capital
   C. increase the total stockholder equity
   D. decrease the book value per share of stock outstanding

16.____

17. The owner of a truck which originally had cost $12,000 but now has a book value of $1,500 was offered $3,000 for it by a used truck dealer. However, the owner traded it in for a new truck listed at $19,000 and received a trade-in allowance of $4,000. The cost basis for the new truck, following the Federal income tax rules, *properly* amounts to

    A. $15,000   B. $16,000   C. $16,500   D. $17,500

18. In planning for purchases to be made during the next month, the following information is to be used:

    Budgeted sales for the month   73,000 units
    Inventory at beginning of the month   19,000 units
    Planned inventory at end of the month   14,000 units

    From the above information, the number of units to be purchased is

    A. 40,000   B. 59,000   C. 68,000   D. 78,000

19. A branch office of a company has the following plan:

    Cash balance at beginning of the month $ 10,000
    Planned cash balance at end of the month $ 15,000
    Expected receipts for the month $ 180,000
    Expected disbursements for the month $ 205,000

    In order to comply with this plan, the accountant should recommend that the branch obtain an additional allocation of

    A. $20,000   B. $25,000   C. $30,000   D. $50,000

20. A company uses the reserve method of bad debt expense and sets up a Bad Debt account at 2% of sales. The sales were $500,000. The company wrote off $7,500 in accounts receivable.
    The effect of these entries on net income for the period is a(n)

    A. $2,500 increase   B. $7,500 decrease
    C. $8,000 decrease   D. $10,000 decrease

KEY (CORRECT ANSWERS)

1. A   11. B
2. C   12. B
3. B   13. D
4. C   14. C
5. D   15. C

6. C   16. D
7. B   17. C
8. A   18. C
9. D   19. C
10. C   20. D

TEST 2

DIRECTIONS: Each question or incomplete statement is followed by several suggested answers or completions. Select the one that BEST answers the question or completes the statement. PRINT THE LETTER OF THE CORRECT ANSWER IN THE SPACE AT THE RIGHT.

1. The Delox Corporation has applied to their bank for a $50,000 loan which they will need for 90 days. The bank grants the loan, which will be discounted at 7% interest. The Delox Corporation will receive credit in their account at the bank for (based on a 360-day year):

    A. $46,500   B. $49,125   C. $50,000   D. $50,875

1.____

Questions 2-5.

DIRECTIONS: Answer Questions 2 through 5 based on the information below.

Assume that you are reviewing some accounts of a company and find the following: The Machinery Account and the Accumulated Depreciation - Machinery Account.

MACHINERY

Jan. 1, 2015	Machine #1	20,000	July 1, 2016	6,000
Jan. 1, 2016	Machine #2	16,000		
July 1, 2016	Machine #3	12,000		
Jan. 1, 2018	Machine #4	20,000		

ACCUMULATED DEPRECIATION - MACHINERY

Dec. 31, 2015	5,000
Dec. 31, 2016	10,500

Machines are depreciated based upon a four-year life and using the straight-line method. Assume no salvage values.

On July 1, 2016, Machine #1, purchased on January 1, 2015, was sold for $6,000 cash. The bookkeeper debited Cash and credited Machinery for $6,000.

On January 1, 2018, Machine #2 was traded in for a newer model. The new Machine had a list price of $34,000. A trade-in value of $10,000 was granted. $20,000 was paid in cash and the bookkeeper debited Machinery and credited Cash for $20,000. Income-tax rules should have been applied making this entry.

If any errors were made in recording the machine values or depreciation, you are asked to correct them and determine the corrected asset values and proper accumulated depreciation.

2. As of December 31, 2015, you determine that these two accounts

    A. are correct
    B. are incorrect
    C. overstate asset book values
    D. understate asset book values

2.____

3. As of December 31, 2016, you determine that, to correct the Machinery Account Balance, you should leave it

    A. unchanged   B. increased by $6,000
    C. decreased by $14,000   D. decreased by $5,500

3.____

4. As of December 31, 2016, you determine that, to reflect the proper balance, the Accumulated Depreciation - Machinery account should

   A. remain unchanged
   B. be increased by $10,000
   C. be decreased by $10,000
   D. be decreased by $ 5,500

5. After the January 1, 2018 entry, you determine that the Machinery Account should, *properly*,

   A. remain unchanged
   B. reflect a corrected balance of $52,000
   C. reflect a corrected balance of $40,000
   D. reflect a corrected balance of $56,000

Questions 6-9.

DIRECTIONS: Answer Questions 6 through 9 based on the information below.

Assume that you are assigned to prepare an Audit Report Summary on the L Company. The L Company uses the accrual method and has an accounting year ending December 31. The bookkeeper of the company has made the following errors:
   1. A $1,500 collection from a customer was received on December 29, 2017, but not recorded until the date of its deposit in the bank, January 4, 2018
   2. A supplier's $1,900 invoice for inventory items received December 2017 was not recorded until January 2018 (Inventories at December 31, 2017 and 2018 were stated correctly, based on physical count)
   3. Depreciation for 2017 was understated by $700
   4. In September 2017, a $350 invoice for office supplies was charged to the Utilities Expense account. Office supplies are expensed as purchased
   5. December 31, 2017, sales on account of $2,500 were recorded in January 2018, although the merchandise had been shipped and was not in the inventory

Assume that no other errors have occurred and that no correcting entries have been made. Ignore all income taxes.

6. After correcting the errors reported above, the corrected Net Income for 2017 was

   A. overstated by $100
   B. understated by $800
   C. understated by $1,800
   D. neither understated nor overstated

7. Working Capital on December 31, 2017 was

   A. understated by $600
   B. understated by $2,300
   C. understated by $1,200
   D. neither understated nor overstated

8. Total Assets on December 31, 2018 were

   A. overstated by $1,100
   B. overstated by $1,800

C. understated by $850
D. neither understated nor overstated

9. The cash balance was

A. correct as stated originally
B. overstated by $1,500
C. understated by $2,500
D. understated by $1,500

Questions 10-13.

DIRECTIONS: Answer Questions 10 through 13 based on the information below.

Salary expense was listed as a total of $27,600 for the month of June 2018. Withholding taxes were determined to be $7,250 for Income taxes and $1,170 for FICA taxes withheld from employees. Payroll deductions for employee pension fund contribution amounted to $2,500.

Assume the employer's FICA tax share is equal to the employees' and that the employer's share of pension costs is double that of the employees and the employer also pays a 3% Unemployment Insurance Tax based upon $20,000 of the wages paid. The employer pays $1,500 for health insurance plans.

10. The amount of cash that must be obtained to meet this net payroll to pay employees is

A. $16,680   B. $19,180   C. $20,350   D. $27,600

11. The total payroll tax expense for this payroll period is

A. $1,170   B. $1,760   C. $2,340   D. $2,940

12. The total liability for withholding and payroll taxes payable is

A. $2,340   B. $7,250   C. $8,420   D. $10,190

13. The expense of the employer for pension and health-care fringe benefits is

A. $1,500   B. $2,500   C. $5,000   D. $6,500

14. Currently preferred terminology for statements to be presented limits the use of the term "reserve" to

A. an actual liability of a known amount
B. estimated liabilities
C. appropriations of retained earnings
D. valuation (contra) accounts

Questions 15-16.

DIRECTIONS: Answer Questions 15 through 16 based on the following.

The Victory Corporation provides an incentive plan whereby its president receives a bonus equal to 10% of the corporate income in excess of $150,000. The bonus is based upon income before income taxes but after calculating the bonus.

15. If the income for the calendar year 2018, before income taxes and before the bonus were $480,000 and the effective tax rate is 40%, the amount of the bonus would be

A. $15,000 B. $30,000 C. $33,000 D. $48,000

16. The income tax expense for calendar year 2012 would be   16.___

   A. $60,000 B. $132,000 C. $180,000 D. $192,000

Questions 17-18.

DIRECTIONS: Answer Questions 17 through 18 based on the information below.

A contract has been awarded to the low bidder. This contractor will then commence construction of a building for the total contract price of $30,000,000. The expected cost of construction is $27,510,000. You are given the additional facts:

	2016	2017	2018
Contract Price as above	$30,000,000	$30,000,000	$30,000,000
Actual Cost to date	$9,170,000	$13,755,000	$27,510,000
Estimated Cost to complete	18,340,000	13,755,000	
Estimated Total Cost	$27,510,000	$27,510,000	$27,510,000
Estimated Total Income	$2,490,000	$	$
Billings	$9,000,000	$9,000,000	$9,000,000

17. For 2016, the income to be recognized on a percentage-of-completion basis would be   17.___

   A. $830,000
   C. $3,000,000
   B. $2,490,000
   D. $9,000,000

18. For 2017, the income to be recognized by the contractor on a percentage-of-completion basis would be   18.___

   A. $415,000 B. $424,500 C. $830,000 D. $1,245,000

19. If the city borrows the $9,000,000 to pay the first billing for the contract above at 10% interest for two years, and the second $9,000,000 at 7% interest for one year, then the interest costs related to this building are, approximately,   19.___

   A. $630,000
   C. $2,430,000
   B. $1,800,000
   D. $3,000,000

20. The books of the Monmouth Corporation show the following: 20.___

	2018	2017	2016
Average earnings for prior 3 years	$70,000	$75,000	$78,000
Net tangible assets	$40,000	$42,000	$50,000

   If it is expected that 15% would be normal earnings on net tangible assets, then the *average* excess earnings are

   A. $7,120 B. $8,333 C. $9,800 D. $10,800

21. A business showed the following figures in its accounts for the year 2018:   21.___
   Sales - $346,000
   Inventory, December 31, 2018 - $58,000
   Inventory, December 31, 2017 - $52,000
   Purchases - $274,000
   Operating Expenses - $36,000
   The gross profit earned by this concern is

   A. $72,000 B. $42,000 C. $66,000 D. $78,000

22. A business firm buys an article for $320, less 40% and 10%, terms 2/10 n/30, on March 18. If it pays the bill on March 27, it should pay

   A. $169.34   B. $172.80   C. $160.00   D. $156.80

23. In the partnership of Danvers and Edwards, Danvers has a capital of $10,000 and Edwards has a capital of $15,000. If Furgal wishes to invest $11,000 and thereby receive a 1/4 interest in the business, the goodwill in the business has been computed to be worth

   A. $19,000   B. $33,000   C. $14,000   D. $8,000

24. George Bailey's capital at the beginning of the year was $14,000. At the end of the year his assets were $62,000 and his liabilities were $39,000. His drawings for the year amounted to $6,000.
   His profit for the year was

   A. $15,000   B. $3,000   C. $9,000   D. $17,000

25. George Wilson's check book shows the following:

   Balance at the beginning of the month   -$3,517.42
   Deposits during the month   -$1,923.98
   Checks drawn during the month   -$2,144.36

   In going over his bank statement, he finds that a deposit of $455.64 made by him has not yet been credited by the bank and that the bank has charged him $9.40 for services rendered. He also finds that he has outstanding checks totaling $268.19.
   His bank statement balance should be printed as

   A. $3,100.19   B. $3,118.99   C. $2,563.81   D. $4,011.47

KEY (CORRECT ANSWERS)

1. B	11. B
2. A	12. D
3. C	13. D
4. C	14. C
5. C	15. B
6. A	16. C
7. A	17. A
8. B	18. A
9. D	19. C
10. A	20. B

21. D
22. A
23. D
24. A
25. A

ACCOUNTING

EXAMINATION SECTION

TEST 1

DIRECTIONS: Each question or incomplete statement is followed by several suggested answers or completions. Select the one that BEST answers the question or completes the statement. *PRINT THE LETTER OF THE CORRECT ANSWER IN THE SPACE AT THE RIGHT.*

Questions 1-5.

DIRECTIONS: Questions 1 through 5 are to be answered on the basis of the following information.

When balance sheets are analyzed, working capital always receives close attention. Adequate working capital enables a company to carry sufficient inventories, meet current debts, take advantage of cash discounts and extend favorable terms to customers. A company that is deficient in working capital and unable to do these things is in a poor competitive position.

Below is a Trial Balance as of June 30, 2021, in alphabetical order, of the Worth Corporation.

	Debits	Credits
Accounts Payable		$50,000
Accounts Receivable	$40,000	
Accrued Expenses Payable		10,000
Capital Stock		10,000
Cash	20,000	
Depreciation Expense	5,000	
Inventory	60,000	
Plant & Equipment (net)	30,000	
Retained Earnings		20,000
Salary Expense	35,000	
Sales		100,000
	$190,000	$190,000

1. The Worth Corporation's Working Capital, based on the data above, is 1._____
   A. $50,000   B. $55,000   C. $60,000   D. $65,000

2. Which one of the following transactions increases Working Capital? 2._____
   A. Collecting outstanding accounts receivable
   B. Borrowing money from the bank based upon a 90-day interest-bearing note payable
   C. Paying off a 60-day note payable to the bank
   D. Selling merchandise at a profit

3. The Worth Corporation's Current Ratio, based on the above data, is   3.____
   A. 1.7 to 1   B. 2 to 1   C. 2.5 to 1   D. 4 to 3

4. Which one of the following transactions decreases the Current Ratio?   4.____
   A. Collecting an account receivable
   B. Borrowing money from the bank giving a 90-day interest-bearing note payable
   C. Paying off a 60-day note payable to the bank
   D. Selling merchandise at a profit

5. The payment of a current liability, such as Payroll Taxes Payable, will   5.____
   A. *increase* the current ratio but have no effect on the working capital
   B. *increase* the Working Capital, but have no effect on the current ratio
   C. *decrease* both the current ratio and working capital
   D. *increase* both the current ratio and working capital

6. During the year 2021, the Ramp Equipment Co. made sales to customers totaling $100,000 that were subject to sales taxes of $8,000. Net cash collections totaled $92,000. Discounts of $3,000 were allowed. During the year 2021, uncollectible accounts in the sum of $2,000 were written off the books.   6.____
   The net change in accounts receivable during the year 2021 was
   A. $10,500   B. $11,000   C. $13,000   D. $13,500

7. The Grable Co. received a $6,000, 8%, 60-day note dated May 1, 2021 from a customer. On May 16, 2021, the Grable Co. discounted the note at 6% at the bank.   7.____
   The net proceeds from the discounting of the note amounted to
   A. $5,954.40   B. $6,034.40   C. $6,064.80   D. $6,080.00

8. In reviewing the customers' accounts in the Accounts Receivable Ledger for the entire year 2020, the following errors are discovered.   8.____
   - A sale in the amount of $500 to the J. Brown Co. was erroneously posted to the K. Brown Co.
   - A sales return of $100 from the Gale Co. was debited to their account.
   - A check was received from a customer, M. White and Co. in payment of a sale of $500 less 2% discount. The check was entered properly in the cash receipts book but was posted to the M. White and Co. account in the amount of $490.

   The difference between the controlling account and its related accounts receivable schedule amounts to
   A. $90   B. $110   C. $190   D. $210

9. Assume that you are called upon to audit a cash fund. You find in the cash drawer postage stamps and I.O.U.'s signed by employees, totaling together $425.   9.____
   In preparing a financial report, the $425 should be reported as
   A. petty cash   B. investments
   C. supplies and receivables   D. cash

10. On December 31, 2020, before adjustment, Accounts Receivable had a debit balance of $60,000 and the Allowance for Uncollectible Accounts had a debit balance of $1,000.
If credit losses are estimated at 5% of Accounts Receivable and the estimated method of reporting bad debts is used, then bad debts expense for the year 2020 would be reported as
A. $1,000   B. $2,000   C. $3,000   D. $4,000

10.____

Questions 11-12.

DIRECTIONS: Questions 11 and 12 are to be answered on the basis of the following information.

Accrued salaries payable on $7,500 had not been recorded on December 31, 2021. Office supplies on hand of $2,500 at December 32, 2021 were erroneously treated as expense instead of inventory. Neither of these errors was discovered or corrected.

11. These two errors would cause the income for 4021 to be
A. *understated* by $5,000
B. *overstated* by $5,000
C. *understated* by $10,000
D. *overstated* by $10,000

11.____

12. The effect of these errors on the retained earnings at December 31, 2021 would be
A. *understated* by $2,500
B. *overstated* by $2,500
C. *understated* by $5,000
D. *overstated* by $5,000

12.____

Questions 13-14.

DIRECTIONS: Questions 13 and 14 are to be answered on the basis of the following information.

Albano, Borrone, and Colluci operate a retail store under the trade name of ABC. Their partnership agreement provides for equaling sharing profits and losses after salaries of $5,000 to Albano, $10,000 to Borrone, and $15,000 to Colluci.

13. If the net income of the partnership (prior to salaries to partners) is $21,000, then Albano's share of the profits, considering all aspects of the agreement, is determined to be
A. $2,000   B. $3,000   C. $5,000   D. $7,000

13.____

14. The share of the profits that apply to Borrone, similarly, is determined to be
A. $2,000   B. $3,000   C. $5,000   D. $7,000

14.____

Questions 15-17.

DIRECTIONS: Questions 15 through 17 are to be answered on the basis of the following information.

4 (#1)

The Kay Company currently uses FIFO for inventory valuation. Their records for the year ended June 30, 2021 reflect the following:

July 1, 2021 inventory	100,000 units @ 7.50
Purchases during year	400,000 units @ $8.00
Sales during year	350,000 units @ $15.00
Expenses exclusive of income taxes	$1,290,000
Cash balance on June 30, 2021	$250,000
Income tax rate	34%

Assume the July 1, 2021 inventory will be the LIFO Base Inventory.

15. If the company should change to the LIFO as of June 30, 2021, then their income before taxes for the year-ended June 30, 2021, as compared with the income FIFO method, will be 15.____
    A. *increased* by $50,000
    B. *decreased* by $50,000
    C. *increased* by $100,000
    D. *decreased* by $100,000

16. Assuming the given tax rate (45%), the use of the LIFO method will result in an approximate tax expense for fiscal 2021 of 16.____
    A. $45,000   B. $50,000   C. $72,000   D. $94,500

17. Assuming the given tax rate (45%), the use of the LIFO inventory method compared with the FIFO method, will result in a change in the approximate income tax expense for fiscal year 2021 as follows: 17.____
    A. *Increase* of $22,500
    B. *Decrease* of $22,500
    C. *Increase* of $45,000
    D. *Decrease* of $45,000

18. An accountant in an agency, in addition to his regular duties, has been assigned to train a newly appointed assistant accountant. The latter believes that he is not being given the training that he needs in order to perform his duties. Accordingly, the MOST appropriate FIRST step for the assistant accountant to take in order to secure the needed training is to 18.____
    A. register for the appropriate courses at the local college as soon as possible
    B. advise the accountant in a formal memo that his apparent lack of interest in the training is impeding his progress
    C. discuss the matter with the accountant privately and try to discover what seems to be the problem
    D. secure such training informally from more sympathetic accountants in the agency

19. You have worked very hard and successfully helped complete a difficult audit of a large corporation doing business with your agency. Your supervisor gives you a brief nod of approval when you expected a more substantial degree of recognition. You are angry and feel unappreciated. 19.____

Of the following, the MOST appropriate course of action for you to take would be to
A. voice your displeasure to your fellow workers at being taken for granted by an unappreciative supervisor
B. say nothing now and assume that your supervisor's nod of approval may be his customary acknowledgment of efforts well done
C. let your supervisor know that he owes you something by repeatedly stressing the outstanding job you've done
D. ease off on your work quality and productivity until your efforts are finally appreciated

20. You have been assisting in an audit of the books and records of businesses as a member of a team. The accountant in charge of your group tells you to start preliminary work independently on a new audit. This audit is to take place at the offices of the business. The business officers have been duly notified of the audit date. Upon arrival at their offices, you find that their records and files are in disarray and that their personnel are antagonistic and uncooperative.
Of the following, the MOST desirable action for you to take is to
A. advise the business officers that serious consequences may follow unless immediate cooperation is secured
B. accept whatever may be shown or told you on the grounds that it would be unwise to further antagonize uncooperative personnel
C. inform your supervisor of the situation and request instructions
D. leave immediately and return later in the expectation of encountering a more cooperative attitude

20.____

KEY (CORRECT ANSWERS)

1.	C	11.	C
2.	D	12.	A
3.	B	13.	A
4.	B	14.	D
5.	A	15.	B
6.	B	16.	C
7.	B	17.	B
8.	D	18.	C
9.	C	19.	B
10.	D	20.	C

TEST 2

DIRECTIONS: Each question or incomplete statement is followed by several suggested answers or completions. Select the one that BEST answers the question or completes the statement. *PRINT THE LETTER OF THE CORRECT ANSWER IN THE SPACE AT THE RIGHT.*

Questions 1-3.

DIRECTIONS: Questions 1 through 3 are to be answered on the basis of the following information.

The city is planning to borrow money with a 5-year, 7% bond issue totaling $10,000,000 on principle when other municipal issues are paying 8%.
Present value of $1 – 8% - 5 years -68057
Present value of annual interest payments – annuity 8% - 5 years – 3.99271

1. The funds obtained from this bond issue (ignoring any costs relating to issuance) would be, approximately,
   A. $9,515,390   B. $10,000,000   C. $10,484,620   D. $10,800,000

   1.____

2. At the date of maturity, the bonds will be redeemed at
   A. $9,515,390   B. $10,000,000   C. $10,484,610   D. $10,800,000

   2.____

3. As a result of this issue, the ACTUAL interest costs each year as related to the 7% interest payments will
   A. be the same as paid ($700,000)
   B. be more than $700,000
   C. be less than $700,000
   D. fluctuate depending on the market conditions

   3.____

4. Following the usual governmental accounting concepts, the activities of a municipal employee retirement plan, which is financed by equal employer and employee contributions, should be accounted for in a(n)
   A. agency fund
   B. intragovernmental service fund
   C. special assessment fund
   D. trust fund

   4.____

Questions 5-7.

DIRECTIONS: Questions 5 through 7 are to be answered on the basis of the following information.

The Balance Sheet of the JLA Corp. is as follows:

Current Assets	$50,000	Current Liabilities	$20,000
Other Assets	75,000	Common Stock	75,000
Total	$125,000	Retained Earnings	30,000
		Total	$125,000

5. The working capital of the JLA Corp. is 5.____
   A. $30,000   B. $50,000   C. $105,000   D. $125,000

6. The operating ratio of the JLA Corp. is 6.____
   A. 2 to 1   B. 2½ to 1   C. 1 to 2   D. 1 to 2½

7. The stockholders' equity is 7.____
   A. $30,000   B. $75,000   C. $105,000   D. $125,000

8. This question is based on the following figures taken from a set of books for the year ending June 30, 2021. 8.____

	Trial Balance Before Adjustments	Trial Balance After Adjustments
Commissions Payable	cr...	cr $1,550
Office Salaries	dr $9,500	dr $10,680
Rental Income	cr $4,300	cr $4,900
Accumulated Depreciation	cr $7,000	cr $9,700
Supplies Expense	dr $1,760	dr $1,200

   As a result of the adjustments reflected in the adjusted trial balance, the net income of the company before taxes will be
   A. *increased* by $4,270
   B. *decreased* by $4,270
   C. *increased* by $5,430
   D. *decreased* by $5,430

9. This question is based on the following facts concerning the operations of a manufacturer of office desks. 9.____

Jan. 1, 2021	Goods in Process Inventory	4,260 units	40% complete
Dec. 31, 2021	Goods in Process Inventory	3,776 units	25% complete
Jan. 1, 2021	Finished Goods Inventory	2,630 units	
Dec. 31, 2021	Finished Goods Inventory	3,180 units	

   Sales consummated during the year: 127,460 units

   Assuming that all the desks are the same style, the number of equivalent complete units, manufactured during the year 2021 is
   A. 127,250   B. 127,460   C. 128,010   D. 131,510

Questions 10-11.

DIRECTIONS: Questions 10 and 11 are to be answered on the basis of the following information.

On January 1, 2021, the Lenox Corporation was organized with a cash investment of $50,000 by the shareholders. Some of the corporate records were destroyed. However, you were able to discover the following facts from various sources.

Accounts Payable at December 31, 2021	$16,000
(arising from merchandise purchased)	
Accounts Receivable at December 31, 2021	$18,000
(arising from the sales of merchandise)	
Sales for the calendar year 2021	$94,000
Inventory, December 31, 2021	20,000
Cost of Goods Sold is 60% of the selling price	
Bank loan outstanding – December 31, 2021	15,000
Expenses paid in cash during the year	35,000
Expenses incurred but unpaid as of December 31, 2021	4,000
Dividend paid	25,000

10. The CORRECT cash balance is 10.____
    A. $5,600   B. $20,600   C. $38,600   D. $40,600

11. The stockholders' equity on December 31, 2021 is 11.____
    A. $23,600   B. Deficit of $26,400
    C. $27,600   D. $42,400

Questions 12-13.

DIRECTIONS: Questions 12 and 13 are to be answered on the basis of the following facts developed from the records of a company that sells its merchandise on the installment plan.

Sales	Calendar Year 2020	Calendar Year 2021
Total volume of sales	$80,000	$100,000
Cost of Goods Sold	60,000	40,000
Gross Profit	$20,000	$60,000
Cash Collections		
From 2020 Sales	$18,000	$36,000
From 2021 Sales		22,000
Total Cash Collections	$18,000	$58,000

12. Using the deferred profit method of determining thee income from installment 12.____
sales, the gross profit on sales for the calendar year 2020 was
    A. $4,500   B. $18,000   C. $20,000   D. None

13. Using the deferred profit method of determining the income from installment 13.____
sales, the gross profit on sales for the calendar year 2021 was
    A. $22,000   B. $22,200   C. $60,000   D. None

Questions 14-15.

DIRECTIONS: Questions 14 and 15 are to be answered on the basis of the data developed from an examination of the records of Ralston, Inc. for the month of April 2021.

4 (#2)

Beginning Inventory: 10,000 units @ $4.00 each

	Purchases		Sales
April 10	20,000 units @ $5 each	April 13	15,000 units @ $8 each
17	60,000 units @ $6 each	21	50,000 units @ $9 each
26	40,000 units @ $7 each	27	50,000 units @ $10 each

14. The gross profit on sales for the month of April, 2021, assuming that inventory is priced on the FIFO basis, is
    A. $330,000   B. $355,000   C. $395,000   D. $435,000

15. The gross profit on sales for the month of April 2021, assuming that inventory is priced on the LIFO basis is
    A. $330,000   B. $355,000   C. $395,000   D. $435,000

16. This question is to be answered on the basis of the data presented for June 30, 2021.

Balance per Bank Statement	$24,019.00
Balance per General Ledger	20,592.64
Proceeds of note collected by the bank which had not been recorded in the Cash account	4,000.00
Interest on note collected by the bank (no book entries made0	39.40
Debit memo for Bank charges for the month of May	23.50
Deposit in Transit (June 30, 2021)	2,144.00
Customer's check returned by the bank due to lack of funds	150.00
Outstanding checks – June 30, 2021	1,631.46
Error in recording check made by our bookkeeper – check cleared in the amount of $463.00 but entered in the bank book for $436.00	

If we wish to reconcile the bank and book balance so that the bank balance and the book balance are reconciled to a corrected balance, the corrected balance should be
    A. $20,592.64   B. $24,019.00   C. $24,531.54   D. $26,163.00

17. The Ateb Company has issued a $500,000 bond issue on January 2, 2021 at 8% interest, payable semi-annually, sold at par, with interest payable on June 30 and December 31.
    On September 30, 2021, at the close of the fiscal year of the Ateb Company, the interest expense accrual should reflect interest payable of, approximately,
    A. $10,000   B. $20,000   C. $40,000   D. $50,000

18. Assume that a new procedure requires that a particular and unvarying sequence of steps be followed in order to yield the desired data. You are assigned to be in charge of subordinates working with this procedure.

Which one of the following is MOST likely to impress subordinates with the importance of following the sequence of steps exactly as given?
- A. Explain the consequences of error if the procedure is not followed.
- B. Suggest how rewarding would be the feeling of finding errors before the supervisor catches them.
- C. Indicate that independent verification of their work will be done by other staff members
- D. Advise that upward career mobility usually results from following instructions exactly

19. It is essential for an experienced accountant to know approximately how long it will take him to complete a particular assignment because
    - A. his supervisors will need to obtain this information only from someone planning to perform the assignment
    - B. he must arrange his schedule to insure proper completion of the assignment consistent with agency objectives
    - C. he must measure whether he is keeping pace with others performing similar assignments
    - D. he must determine what assignments are essential and have the greatest priority within his agency

20. There are circumstances which call for special and emergency efforts by employees. You must assign your staff to make this type of effort.
    Of the following, this special type of assignment is MOST likely to succeed if the
    - A. time schedule required to complete the assignment is precisely stated but is not adhered to
    - B. employees are individually free to determine the work schedule
    - C. assignment is clearly defined
    - D. employees are individually free to use any procedure or method available to them

KEY (CORRECT ANSWERS)

1.	A	11.	A
2.	B	12.	A
3.	B	13.	B
4.	D	14.	C
5.	A	15.	B
6.	B	16.	C
7.	C	17.	A
8.	B	18.	A
9.	A	19.	B
10.	B	20.	C

INTERPRETING STATISTICAL DATA
GRAPHS, CHARTS AND TABLES
EXAMINATION SECTION
TEST 1

DIRECTIONS: Each questioner incomplete statement is followed by several suggested answers or completions. Select the one that BEST answers the question or completes the statement. *PRINT THE LETTER OF THE CORRECT ANSWER IN THE SPACE AT THE RIGHT.*

Questions 1-3.

DIRECTIONS: Questions 1 through 3 are to be answered SOLELY on the basis of the following table.

QUARTERLY SALES REPORTED BY MAJOR INDUSTRY GROUPS

DECEMBER 2021 – FEBRUARY 2023
Reported Sales, Taxable & Non-Taxable (in Millions)

Industry Groups	12/21-2/22	3/22-5/22	6/22-8/22	9/22-11/22	12/22-2/23
Retailers	2,802	2,711	2,475	2,793	2,974
Wholesalers	2,404	2,237	2,269	2,485	2,974
Manufacturers	3,016	2,888	3,001	3,518	3,293
Services	1,034	1,065	984	1,132	1,092

1. The trend in total reported sales may be described as

   A. downward
   B. downward and upward
   C. horizontal
   D. upward

2. The two industry groups that reveal a similar seasonal pattern for the period December 2021 through November 2022 are

   A. retailers and manufacturers
   B. retailers and wholesalers
   C. wholesalers and manufacturers
   D. wholesalers and service

3. Reported sales were at a MINIMUM between

   A. December 2021 and February 2022
   B. March 2022 and May 2022
   C. June 2022 and August 2022
   D. September 2022 and November 2022

TEST 2

DIRECTIONS: Each question or incomplete statement is followed by several suggested answers or completions. Select the one that BEST answers the question or completes the statement. *PRINT THE LETTER OF THE CORRECT ANSWER IN THE SPACE AT THE RIGHT*

Questions 1-4.

DIRECTIONS: Questions 1 through 4 are to be answered SOLELY on the basis of the following information.

The income elasticity of demand for selected items of consumer demand in the United States are:

Item	Elasticity
Airline Travel	5.66
Alcohol	.62
Dentist Fees	1.00
Electric Utilities	3.00
Gasoline	1.29
Intercity Bus	1.89
Local Bus	1.41
Restaurant Meals	.75

1. The demand for the item listed below that would be MOST adversely affected by a decrease in income is

   A. alcohol
   B. electric utilities
   C. gasoline
   D. restaurant meals

2. The item whose relative change in demand would be the same as the relative change in income would be

   A. dentist fees
   B. gasoline
   C. restaurant meals
   D. none of the above

3. If income increases by 12 percent, the demand for restaurant meals may be expected to increase by

   A. 9 percent
   B. 12 percent
   C. 16 percent
   D. none of the above

4. On the basis of the above information, the item whose demand would be MOST adversely affected by an increase in the sales tax from 7 percent to 8 percent to be passed on to the consumer in the form of higher prices

   A. would be airline travel
   B. would be alcohol
   C. would be gasoline
   D. cannot be determined

TEST 3

DIRECTIONS: Each question or incomplete statement is followed by several suggested answers or completions. Select the one that BEST answers the question or completes the statement. *PRINT THE LETTER OF THE CORRECT ANSWER IN THE SPACE AT THE RIGHT.*

Questions 1-3.

DIRECTIONS: Questions 1 through 3 are to be answered SOLELY on the basis of the following graphs depicting various relationships in a single retail store.

GRAPH 1
RELATIONSHIP BETWEEN NUMBER OF CUSTOMERS STORE AND TIME OF DAY

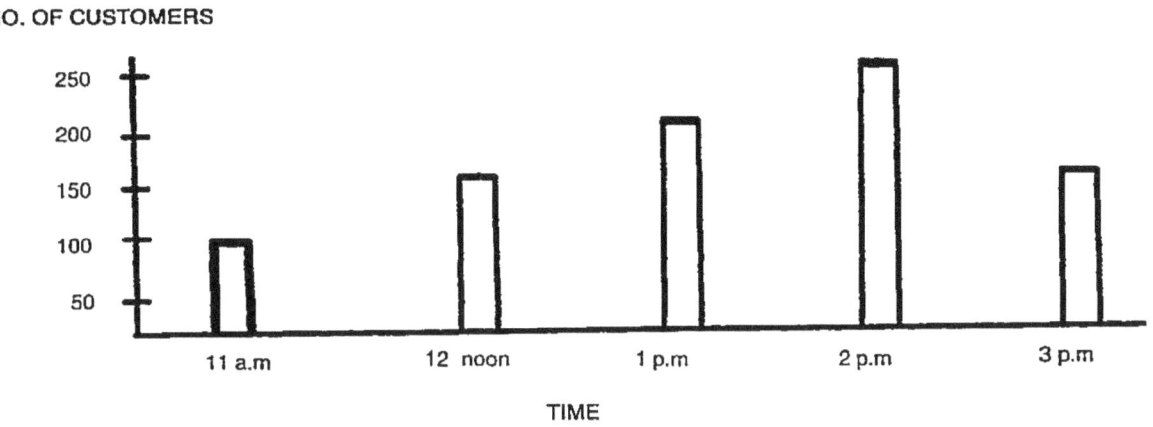

GRAPH II
RELATIONSHIP BETWEEN NUMBER OF CHECK-OUT LANES AVAILABLE IN STORE AND WAIT TIME FOR CHECK-OUT

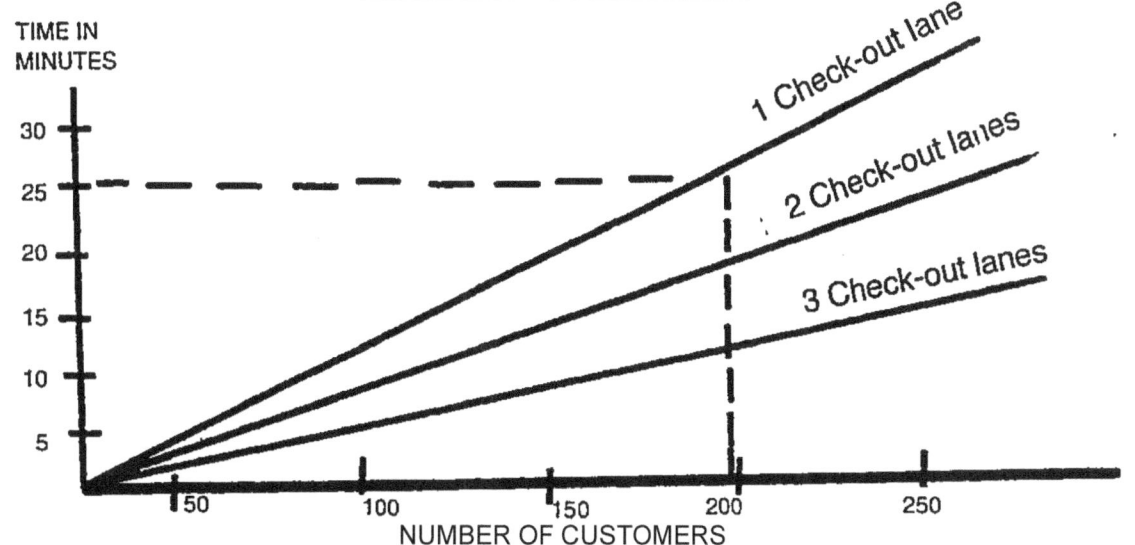

Note the dotted lines in Graph II. They demonstrate that, if there are 200 people in the store and only one check-out lane is open, the wait time will be 25 minutes.

85

1. At what time would a person be most likely NOT to have to wait more than 15 minutes if only one check-out lane is open?

   A. 11 A.M. B. 12 Noon C. 1 P.M. D. 3 P.M.

2. At what time of day would a person have to wait the LONGEST to check out if three check-out lanes are available?

   A. 11 A.M. B. 12 Noon C. 1 P.M. D. 2 P.M

3. The difference in wait times between 1 and 3 check-out lanes at 3 P.M. is MOST NEARLY

   A. 5 B. 10 C. 15 D. 20

———

TEST 4

DIRECTIONS: Each question or incomplete statement is followed by several suggested answers or completions. Select the one that BEST answers the question or completes the statement. *PRINT THE LETTER OF THE CORRECT ANSWER IN THE SPACE AT THE RIGHT.*

Questions 1-4.

DIRECTIONS: Questions 1 through 4 are to be answered SOLELY on the basis of the graph below.

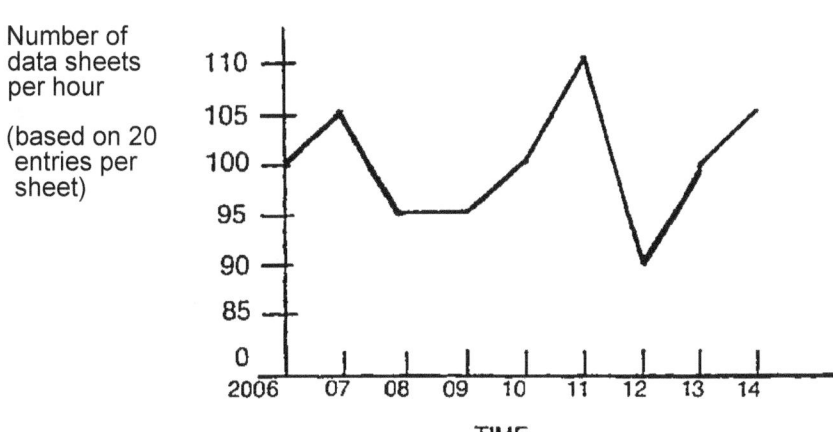

1. Of the following, during what four-year period did the average output of computer operators fall BELOW 100 sheets per hour?

   A. 2007-10   B. 2008-11   C. 2010-13   D. 2011-14

2. The average percentage change in output over the previous year's output for the years 2009 to 2012 is MOST NEARLY

   A. 2   B. 0   C. -5   D. -7

3. The difference between the actual output for 2012 and the projected figure based upon the average increase from 2006-2011 is MOST NEARLY

   A. 18   B. 20   C. 22   D. 24

4. Assume that after constructing the above graph you, an analyst, discovered that the average number of entries per sheet in 2012 was 25 (instead of 20) because of the complex nature of the work performed during that period.
   The average output in sheets per hour for the period 2010-13, expressed in terms of 20 items per sheet, would then be MOST NEARLY

   A. 95   B. 100   C. 105   D. 110

TEST 6

DIRECTIONS: Each question or incomplete statement is followed by several suggested answers or completions. Select the one that BEST answers the question or completes the statement. *PRINT THE LETTER OF THE CORRECT ANSWER IN THE SPACE AT THE RIGHT.*

Questions 1-3.

DIRECTIONS: Questions 1 through 3 are to be answered on the basis of the following data assembled for a cost-benefit analysis.

	Cost	Benefit
No program	0	0
Alternative W	$ 3,000	$ 6,000
Alternative X	$10,000	$17,000
Alternative Y	$17,000	$25,000
Alternative Z	$30,000	$32,000

1. From the point of view of selecting the alternative with the best cost benefit ratio, the BEST alternative is Alternative

    A. W B. X C. Y D. Z

2. From the point of view of selecting the alternative with the best measure of net benefit, the BEST alternative is Alternative

    A. W B. X C. Y D. Z

3. From the point of view of pushing public expenditure to the point where marginal benefit equals or exceeds marginal cost, the BEST alternative is Alternative

    A. W B. X C. Y D. Z

TEST 6

DIRECTIONS: Each question or incomplete statement is followed by several suggested answers or completions. Select the one that BEST answers the question or completes the statement. *PRINT THE LETTER OF THE CORRECT ANSWER IN THE SPACE AT THE RIGHT.*

Questions 1-3.

DIRECTIONS: Questions 1 through 3 are to be answered SOLELY on the basis of the following data.

A series of cost-benefit studies of various alternative health programs yields the following results:

Program	Benefit	Cost
K	30	15
L	60	60
M	300	150
N	600	500

In answering Questions 1 and 2, assume that all programs can be increased or decreased in scale without affecting their individual benefit-to-cost ratios.

1. The benefit-to-cost ratio of Program M is

   A. 10:1   B. 5:1   C. 2:1   D. 1:2

2. The budget ceiling for one or more of the programs included in the study is set at 75 units. It may MOST logically be concluded that

   A. Programs K and L should be chosen to fit within the budget ceiling
   B. Program K would be the most desirable one that could be afforded
   C. Program M should be chosen rather than Program K
   D. the choice should be between Programs M and K

3. If no assumptions can be made regarding the effects of change of scale, the MOST logical conclusion, on the basis of the data available, is that

   A. more data are needed for a budget choice of program
   B. Program K is the most preferable because of its low cost and good benefit-to-cost ratio
   C. Program M is the most preferable because of its high benefits and good benefit-to-cost ratio
   D. there is no difference between Programs K and M, and either can be chosen for any purpose

TEST 7

DIRECTIONS: Each question or incomplete statement is followed by several suggested answers or completions. Select the one that BEST answers the question or completes the statement. *PRINT THE LETTER OF THE CORRECT ANSWER IN THE SPACE AT THE RIGHT.*

Questions 1-6.

DIRECTIONS: Questions 1 through 6 are to be answered SOLELY on the basis of the information contained in the charts below which relate to the budget allocations of City X, a small suburban community. The charts depict the annual budget allocations by Department and by expenditures over a five-year period.

CITY X BUDGET IN MILLIONS OF DOLLARS
TABLE I. Budget Allocations by Department

Department	2017	2018	2019	2020	2021
Public Safety	30	45	50	40	50
Health and Welfare	50	75	90	60	70
Engineering	5	8	10	5	8
Human Resources	10	12	20	10	22
Conservation & Environment	10	15	20	20	15
Education & Development	15	25	35	15	15
TOTAL BUDGET	120	180	225	150	180

TABLE II. Budget Allocations by Expenditures

Category	2017	2018	2019	2020	2021
Raw Materials & Machinery	36	63	68	30	98
Capital Outlay	12	27	56	15	18
Personal Services	72	90	101	105	64
TOTAL BUDGET	120	180	225	150	180

1. The year in which the SMALLEST percentage of the total annual budget was allocated to the Department of Education and Development is

   A. 2017   B. 2018   C. 2020   D. 2021

2. Assume that in 2020 the Department of Conservation and Environment divided its annual budget into the three categories of expenditures and in exactly the same proportion as the budget shown in Table II for the year 2020. The amount allocated for capital outlay in the Department of Conservation and Environment's 2020 budget was MOST NEARLY _____ million.

   A. $2   B. $4   C. $6   D. $10

3. From the year 2018 to the year 2020, the sum of the annual budgets for the Departments of Public Safety and Engineering showed an overall _____ million.

   A. decline; SB
   B. increase; $7
   C. decline; S15
   D. increase; S22

4. The LARGEST dollar increase in departmental budget allocations from one year to the next was in _____ from _____.

   A. Public Safety; 2017 to 2018
   B. Health and Welfare; 2017 to 2018
   C. Education and Development; 2019 to 2020
   D. Human Resources; 2019 to 2020

5. During the five-year period, the annual budget of the Department of Human Resources was GREATER than the annual budget for the Department of Conservation and Environment in _____ of the years.

   A. none
   B. one
   C. two
   D. three

6. If the total City X budget increases at the same rate from 2021 to 2022 as it did from 2020 to 2021, the total City X budget for 2022 will be MOST NEARLY _____ million.

   A. $180
   B. $200
   C. $210
   D. $215

TEST 8

DIRECTIONS: Each question or incomplete statement is followed by several suggested answers or completions. Select the one that BEST answers the question or completes the statement. *PRINT THE LETTER OF THE CORRECT ANSWER IN THE SPACE AT THE RIGHT.*

Questions 1-3.

DIRECTIONS: Questions 1 through 3 are to be answered SOLELY on the basis of the following information.

Assume that in order to encourage Program A, the State and Federal governments have agreed to make the following reimbursements for money spent on Program A, provided the unreimbursed balance is paid from City funds.

During Fiscal Year 2021-2022 - For the first $2 million expended, 50% Federal reimbursement and 30% State reimbursement; for the next $3 million, 40% Federal reimbursement and 20% State reimbursement; for the next $5 million, 20% Federal reimbursement and 10% State reimbursement. Above $10 million expended, no Federal or State reimbursement.

During Fiscal Year 2022-2023 - For the first $1 million expended, 30% Federal reimbursement and 20% State reimbursement; for the next $4 million, 15% Federal reimbursement and 10% State reimbursement. Above $5 million expended, no Federal or State reimbursement.

1. Assume that the Program A expenditures are such that the State reimbursement for Fiscal Year 2021-2022 will be $1 million.
   Then, the Federal reimbursement for Fiscal Year 2021-2022 will be

   A. $1,600,000   B. $1,800,000
   C. $2,000,000   D. $2,600,000

2. Assume that $8 million were to be spent on Program A in Fiscal Year 2022-2023.
   The TOTAL amount of unreimbursed City funds required would be

   A. $3,500,000   B. $4,500,000
   C. $5,500,000   D. $6,500,000

3. Assume that the City desires to have a combined total of $6 million spent in Program A during both the Fiscal Year 2021-2022 and the Fiscal Year 2022-2023.
   Of the following expenditure combinations, the one which results in the GREATEST reimbursement of City funds is _____ in Fiscal Year 2021-2022 and _____ in Fiscal Year 2022-2023.

   A. $5 million; $1 million   B. $4 million; $2 million
   C. $3 million; $3 million   D. $2 million; $4 million

KEY (CORRECT ANSWERS)

TEST 1

1. D
2. C
3. C

TEST 2

1. B
2. A
3. A
4. D

TEST 3

1. A
2. D
3. B

TEST 4

1. A
2. B
3. C
4. C

TEST 5

1. A
2. C
3. C

TEST 6

1. C
2. D
3. A

TEST 7

1. D
2. A
3. A
4. B
5. B
6. D

TEST 8

1. B
2. D
3. A

PREPARING WRITTEN MATERIAL
EXAMINATION SECTION
TEST 1

DIRECTIONS: Each of the sentences in this test may be classified under one of the following four categories:
    A. *Incorrect* because of faulty grammar or sentence structure
    B. *Incorrect* because of faulty punctuation
    C. *Incorrect* because of faulty capitalization
    D. *Correct*

Examine each sentence carefully to determine under which of the above four options it is best classified. Then, in the space at the right, print the capital letter preceding the option which is the BEST of the four suggested above.

(Each incorrect sentence contains but one type of error. Consider a sentence to be correct if it contains none of the types of errors mentioned, even though there may be other correct ways of expressing the same thought.)

1. This fact, together with those brought out at the previous meeting, prove that the schedule is satisfactory to the employees.   1.____

2. Like many employees in scientific fields, the work of bookkeepers and accountants requires accuracy and neatness.   2.____

3. "What can I do for you," the secretary asked as she motioned to the visitor to take a seat.   3.____

4. Our representative, Mr. Charles will call on you next week to determine whether or not your claim has merit.   4.____

5. We expect you to return in the spring; please do not disappoint us.   5.____

6. Any supervisor, who disregards the just complaints of his subordinates, is remiss in the performance of his duty.   6.____

7. Because she took less than an hour for lunch is no reason for permitting her to leave before five o'clock.   7.____

8. "Miss Smith," said the supervisor, "Please arrange a meeting of the staff for two o'clock on Monday."   8.____

9. A private company's vacation and sick leave allowance usually differs considerably from a public agency.   9.____

10. Therefore, in order to increase the efficiency of operations in the department, a report on the recommended changes in procedures was presented to the departmental committee in charge of the program.   10.____

11. We told him to assign the work to whoever was available. 11.____

12. Since John was the most efficient of any other employee in the bureau, he received the highest service rating. 12.____

13. Only those members of the national organization who resided in the middle West attended the conference in Chicago. 13.____

14. The question of whether the office manager has as yet attained, or indeed can ever hope to secure professional status is one which has been discussed for years. 14.____

15. No one knew who to blame for the error which, we later discovered, resulted in a considerable loss of time. 15.____

KEY (CORRECT ANSWERS)

1.	A	6.	B	11.	D
2.	A	7.	A	12.	A
3.	B	8.	C	13.	C
4.	B	9.	A	14.	B
5.	D	10.	D	15.	A

TEST 2

DIRECTIONS: Each of the sentences in this test may be classified under one of the following four categories:
- A. *Incorrect* because of faulty grammar or sentence structure
- B. *Incorrect* because of faulty punctuation
- C. *Incorrect* because of faulty capitalization
- D. *Correct*

1. The National alliance of Businessmen is trying to persuade private businesses to hire youth in the summertime.   1.____

2. The supervisor who is on vacation, is in charge of processing vouchers.   2.____

3. The activity of the committee at its conferences is always stimulating.   3.____

4. After checking the addresses again, the letters went to the mailroom.   4.____

5. The director, as well as the employees, are interested in sharing the dividends.   5.____

KEY (CORRECT ANSWERS)

1. C
2. B
3. D
4. A
5. A

TEST 3

DIRECTIONS: In each of the following groups of sentences, one of the four sentences is faulty in grammar, punctuation, or capitalization. Select the INCORRECT sentence in each case.

1. A. Sailing down the bay was a thrilling experience for me.
   B. He was not consulted about your joining the club.
   C. This story is different than the one I told you yesterday.
   D. There is no doubt about his being the best player.

   1.____

2. A. He maintains there is but one road to world peace.
   B. It is common knowledge that a child sees much he is not supposed to see.
   C. Much of the bitterness might have been avoided if arbitration had been resorted to earlier in the meeting.
   D. The man decided it would be advisable to marry a girl somewhat younger than him.

   2.____

3. A. In this book, the incident I liked least is where the hero tries to put out the forest fire.
   B. Learning a foreign language will undoubtedly give a person a better understanding of his mother tongue.
   C. His actions made us wonder what he planned to do next.
   D. Because of the war, we were unable to travel during the summer vacation.

   3.____

4. A. The class had no sooner become interested in the lesson than the dismissal bell rang.
   B. There is little agreement about the kind of world to be planned at the peace conference.
   C. "Today," said the teacher, "we shall read 'The Wind in the Willows,' I am sure you'll like it.
   D. The terms of the legal settlement of the family quarrel handicapped both sides for many years.

   4.____

5. A. I was so surprised that I was not able to say a word.
   B. She is taller than any other member of the class.
   C. It would be much more preferable if you were never seen in his company.
   D. We had no choice but to excuse her for being late.

   5.____

KEY (CORRECT ANSWERS)

1. C
2. D
3. A
4. C
5. C

TEST 4

DIRECTIONS: In each of the following groups of sentences, one of the four sentences is faulty in grammar, punctuation, or capitalization. Select the INCORRECT sentence in each case.

1. A. Please send me these data at the earliest opportunity.
    B. The loss of their material proved to be a severe handicap.
    C. My principal objection to this plan is that it is impracticable.
    D. The doll had laid in the rain for an hour and was ruined.

2. A. The garden scissors, left out all night in the rain, were in a badly rusted condition.
    B. The girls felt bad about the misunderstanding which had arisen
    C. Sitting near the campfire, the old man told John and I about many exciting adventures he had had.
    D. Neither of us is in a position to undertake a task of that magnitude.

3. A. The general concluded that one of the three roads would lead to the besieged city.
    B. The children didn't, as a rule, do hardly anything beyond what they were told to do.
    C. The reason the girl gave for her negligence was that she had acted on the spur of the moment.
    D. The daffodils and tulips look beautiful in that blue vase.

4. A. If I was ten years older, I should be interested in this work.
    B. Give the prize to whoever has drawn the best picture.
    C. When you have finished reading the book, take it back to the library.
    D. My drawing is as good as or better than yours.

5. A. He asked me whether the substance was animal or vegetable.
    B. An apple which is unripe should not be eaten by a child.
    C. That was an insult to me who am your friend.
    D. Some spy must of reported the matter to the enemy.

6. A. Limited time makes quoting the entire message impossible.
    B. Who did she say was going?
    C. The girls in your class have dressed more dolls this year than we.
    D. There was such a large amount of books on the floor that I couldn't find a place for my rocking chair.

7. A. What with his sleeplessness and his ill health, he was unable to assume any responsibility for the success of the meeting.
    B. If I had been born in February, I should be celebrating my birthday soon.
    C. In order to prevent breakage, she placed a sheet of paper between each of the plates when she packed them.
    D. After the spring shower, the violets smelled very sweet.

8. A. He had laid the book down very reluctantly before the end of the lesson.
    B. The dog, I am sorry to say, had lain on the bed all night.
    C. The cloth was first lain on a flat surface; then it was pressed with a hot iron.
    D. While we were in Florida, we lay in the sun until we were noticeably tanned.

9. A. If John was in New York during the recent holiday season, I have no doubt he spent most of the time with his parents.
    B. How could he enjoy the television program; the dog was barking and the baby was crying.
    C. When the problem was explained to the class, he must have been asleep.
    D. She wished that her new dress were finished so that she could go to the party.

10. A. The engine not only furnishes power but light and heat as well.
    B. You're aware that we've forgotten whose guilt was established, aren't you?
    C. Everybody knows that the woman made many sacrifices for her children.
    D. A man with his dog and gun is a familiar sight in this neighborhood.

KEY (CORRECT ANSWERS)

1.	D	6.	D
2.	C	7.	B
3.	B	8.	C
4.	A	9.	B
5.	D	10.	A

TEST 5

DIRECTIONS: Each of Questions 1 through 5 consists of a sentence which may be classified appropriately under one of the following four categories:
  A. *Incorrect* because of faulty grammar
  B. *Incorrect* because of faulty punctuation
  C. *Incorrect* because of faulty spelling
  D. *Correct*

Examine each sentence carefully. Then, print in the space at the right the letter preceding the category which is the BEST of the four suggested above
(Note: Each incorrect sentence contains only one type of error. Consider a sentence correct if it contains no errors, although there may be other correct ways of writing the sentence.)

1. Of the two employees, the one in our office is the most efficient. 1.____

2. No one can apply or even understand, the new rules and regulations. 2.____

3. A large amount of supplies were stored in the empty office. 3.____

4. If an employee is occassionally asked to work overtime, he should do so willingly. 4.____

5. It is true that the new procedures are difficult to use but, we are certain that you will learn them quickly. 5.____

6. The office manager said that he did not know who would be given a large allotment under the new plan. 6.____

7. It was at the supervisor's request that the clerk agreed to postpone his vacation. 7.____

8. We do not believe that it is necessary for both he and the clerk to attend the conference. 8.____

9. All employees, who display perseverance, will be given adequate recognition. 9.____

10. He regrets that some of us employees are dissatisfied with our new assignments. 10.____

11. "Do you think that the raise was merited," asked the supervisor? 11.____

12. The new manual of procedure is a valuable supplement to our rules and regulations. 12.____

13. The typist admitted that she had attempted to pursuade the other employees to assist her in her work. 13.____

14. The supervisor asked that all amendments to the regulations be handled by you and I.   14.____

15. The custodian seen the boy who broke the window.   15.____

KEY (CORRECT ANSWERS)

1. A   6. D   11. B
2. B   7. D   12. C
3. A   8. A   13. C
4. C   9. B   14. A
5. B   10. D 15. A

REPORT WRITING

EXAMINATION SECTION

TEST 1

DIRECTIONS: Each question or incomplete statement is followed by several suggested answers or completions. Select the one that BEST answers the question or completes the statement. *PRINT THE LETTER OF THE CORRECT ANSWER IN THE SPACE AT THE RIGHT.*

Questions 1-4.

DIRECTIONS: Answer Questions 1 through 4 on the basis of the following report which was prepared by a supervisor for inclusion in his agency's annual report.

Line #
1   On Oct. 13, I was assigned to study the salaries paid.
2   to clerical employees in various titles by the city and by
3   private industry in the area.
4   In order to get the data I needed, I called Mr. Johnson at
5   the Bureau of the Budget and the payroll officers at X Corp.—
6   a brokerage house, Y Co. —an insurance company, and Z Inc. —
7   a publishing firm. None of them was available and I had to call
8   all of them again the next day.
9   When I finally got the information I needed, I drew up a
10 chart, which is attached. Note that not all of the companies I
11 contacted employed people at all the different levels used in the
12 city service.
13 The conclusions I draw from analyzing this information is
14 as follows: The city's entry-level salary is about average for
15 the region; middle-level salaries are generally higher in the
16 city government plan than in private industry; but salaries at the
17 highest levels in private industry are better than city em-
18 ployees' pay.

1. Which of the following criticisms about the style in which this report is written is MOST valid?
   A. It is too informal.
   B. It is too concise.
   C. It is too choppy.
   D. The syntax is too complex.

   1._____

2. Judging from the statements made in the report, the method followed by this employee in performing his research was
   A. *good*; he contacted a representative sample of businesses in the area
   B. *poor*; he should have drawn more definite conclusions
   C. *good*; he was persistent in collecting information
   D. *poor*; he did not make a thorough study

   2._____

3. One sentence in this report contains a grammatical error. This sentence begins on line number
   A. 4   B. 7   C. 10   D. 14

4. The type of information given in this report which should be presented in footnotes or in an appendix is the
   A. purpose of the study
   B. specifics about the businesses contacted
   C. reference to the chart
   D. conclusions drawn by the author

5. The use of a graph to show statistical data in a report is SUPERIOR to a table because it
   A. features approximations
   B. emphasizes facts and relationships more dramatically
   C. presents data more accurately
   D. is easily understood by the average reader

6. Of the following, the degree of formality required of a written report in tone is MOST likely to depend on the
   A. subject matter of the report
   B. frequency of its occurrence
   C. amount of time available for its preparation
   D. audience for whom the report is intended

7. Of the following, a distinguishing characteristic of a written report intended for the head of your agency as compared to a report prepared for a lower-echelon staff member is that the report for the agency head should USUALLY include
   A. considerably more detail, especially statistical data
   B. the essential details in an abbrevated form
   C. all available source material
   D. an annotated bibliography

8. Assume that you are asked to write a lengthy report for use by the administrator of your agency, the subject of which is "The Impact of Proposed New Data Processing Operation on Line Personnel" in your agency. You decide that the *most* appropriate type of report for you to prepare is an analytical report, including recommendations.
   The MAIN reason for your decision is that
   A. the subject of the report is extremely complex
   B. large sums of money are involved
   C. the report is being prepared for the administrator
   D. you intend to include charts and graphs

9. Assume that you are preparing a report based on a survey dealing with the attitudes of employees in Division X regarding proposed new changes in compensating employees for working overtime. Three percent of the respondents to the survey voluntarily offer an unfavorable opinion on the method of assigning overtime work, a question not specifically asked of the employees.
On the basis of this information, the MOST appropriate and significant of the following comments for you to make in the report with regard to employees' attitudes on assigning overtime work is that
    A. an insignificant percentage of employees dislike the method of assigning overtime work
    B. three percent of the employees in Division X dislike the method of assigning overtime work
    C. three percent of the sample selected for the survey voiced an unfavorable opinion on the method of assigning overtime work
    D. some employees voluntarily voiced negative feelings about the method of assigning overtime work, making it impossible to determine the extent of this attitude

9.____

10. A supervisor should be able to prepare a report that is well-written and unambiguous.
Of the following sentences that might appear in a report, select the one which communicates MOST clearly the intent of its author.
    A. When your subordinates speak to a group of people, they should be well-informed.
    B. When he asked him to leave, SanMan King told him that he would refuse the request.
    C. Because he is a good worker, Foreman Jefferson assigned Assistant Foreman D'Agostino to replace him.
    D. Each of us is responsible for the actions of our subordinates.

10.____

11. In some reports, especially longer ones, a list of the resources (books, papers, magazines, etc.) used to prepare it is included. This list is called the
    A. accreditation   B. bibliography
    C. summary   D. glossary

11.____

12. Reports are usually divided into several sections, some of which are more necessary than others.
Of the following, the section which is ABSOLUTELY necessary to include in a report is
    A. a table of contents   B. the body
    C. an index   D. a bibliography

12.____

13. Suppose you are writing a report on an interview you have just completed with a particularly hostile applicant.
    Which of the following BEST describes what you should include in this report?
    A. What you think caused the applicant's hostile attitude during the interview
    B. Specific examples of the applicant's hostile remarks and behavior
    C. The relevant information uncovered during the interview
    D. A recommendation that the applicant's request be denied because of his hostility

13.____

14. When including recommendations in a report to your supervisor, which of the following is MOST important for you to do?
    A. Provide several alternative courses of action for each recommendation
    B. First present the supporting evidence, then the recommendations
    C. First present the recommendations, then the supporting evidence
    D. Make sure the recommendations arise logically out of the information in the report

14.____

15. It is often necessary that the writer of a report present facts and sufficient arguments to gain acceptance of the points, conclusions, or recommendations set forth in the report.
    Of the following, the LEAST advisable step to take in organizing a report, when such argumentation is the important factor, is a(n)
    A. elaborate expression of personal belief
    B. businesslike discussion of the problem as a whole
    C. orderly arrangement of convincing data
    D. reasonable explanation of the primary issues

15.____

16. In some types of reports, visual aids add interest, meaning, and support. They also provide an essential means of effectively communicating the message of the report.
    Of the following, the selection of the suitable visual aids to use with a report is LEAST dependent on the
    A. nature and scope of the report
    B. way in which the aid is to be used
    C. aid used in other reports
    D. prospective readers of the report

16.____

17. Visual aids used in a report may be placed either in the text material or in the appendix.
    Deciding where to put a chart, table, or any such aid should depend on the
    A. title of the report   B. purpose of the visual aid
    C. title of the visual aid   D. length of the report

17.____

18. A report is often revised several times before final preparation and distribution in an effort to make certain the report meets the needs of the situation for which it is designed.
    Which of the following is the BEST way for the author to be sure that a report covers the areas he intended?

18.____

A. Obtain a coworker's opinion
B. Compare it with a content checklist
C. Test it on a subordinate
D. Check his bibliography

19. In which of the following situations is an oral report preferable to a written report? When a(n)
    A. recommendation is being made for a future plan of action
    B. department head requests immediate information
    C. long-standing policy change is made
    D. analysis of complicated statistical data is involved

20. When an applicant is approved, the supervisor must fill in standard forms with certain information.
    The GREATEST advantage of using standard forms in this situation rather than having the supervisor write the report as he sees fit is that
    A. the report can be acted on quickly
    B. the report can be written without directions from a supervisor
    C. needed information is less likely to be left out of the report
    D. information that is written up this way is more likely to be verified

21. Assume that it is part of your job to prepare a monthly report for your unit head that eventually goes to the director. The report contains information on the number of applicants you have interviewed that have been approved and the number of applicants you have interviewed that have been turned down.
    Errors on such reports are serious because
    A. you are expected to be able to prove how many applicants you have interviewed each month
    B. accurate statistics are needed for effective management of the department
    C. they may not be discovered before the report is transmitted to the director
    D. they may result in loss to the applicants left out of the report

22. The frequency with which job reports are submitted should depend MAINLY on
    A. how comprehensive the report has to be
    B. the amount of information in the report
    C. the availability of an experienced man to write the report
    D. the importance of changes in the information included in the report

23. The CHIEF purpose in preparing an outline for a report is usually to insure that
    A. the report will be grammatically correct
    B. every point will be given equal emphasis
    C. principal and secondary points will be properly integrated
    D. the language of the report will be of the same level and include the same technical terms

24. The MAIN reason for requiring written job reports is to
    A. avoid the necessity of oral orders
    B. develop better methods of doing the work
    C. provide a permanent record of what was done
    D. increase the amount of work that can be done

25. Assume you are recommending in a report to your supervisor that a radical change in a standard maintenance procedure should be adopted.
    Of the following, the MOST important information to be included in this report is
    A. a list of the reasons for making this change
    B. the names of others who favor the change
    C. a complete description of the present procedure
    D. amount of training time needed for the new procedure

KEY (CORRECT ANSWERS)

1.	A		11.	B
2.	D		12.	B
3.	D		13.	C
4.	B		14.	D
5.	B		15.	A
6.	D		16.	C
7.	B		17.	B
8.	A		18.	B
9.	D		19.	B
10.	D		20.	C

21. B
22. D
23. C
24. C
25. A

TEST 2

DIRECTIONS: Each question or incomplete statement is followed by several suggested answers or completions. Select the one that BEST answers the question or completes the statement. *PRINT THE LETTER OF THE CORRECT ANSWER IN THE SPACE AT THE RIGHT.*

1. It is often necessary that the writer of a report present facts and sufficient arguments to gain acceptance of the points, conclusions, or recommendations set forth in the report.
Of the following, the LEAST advisable step to take in organizing a report, when such argumentation is the important factor, is a(n)
    A. elaborate expression of personal belief
    B. businesslike discussion of the problem as a whole
    C. orderly arrangement of convincing data
    D. reasonable explanation of the primary issues

    1.____

2. Of the following, the factor which is generally considered to be LEAST characteristic of a good control report is that it
    A. stresses performance that adheres to standard rather than emphasizing the exception
    B. supplies information intended to serve as the basis for corrective action
    C. provides feedback for the planning process
    D. includes data that reflect trends as well as current status

    2.____

3. An administrative assistant has been asked by his superior to write a concise, factual report with objective conclusions and recommendations based on facts assembled by other researchers.
Of the following factors, the administrative assistant should give LEAST consideration to
    A. the educational level of the person or persons for whom the report is being prepared
    B. the use to be made of the report
    C. the complexity of the problem
    D. his own feelings about the importance of the problem

    3.____

4. When making a written report, it is often recommended that the findings or conclusions be presented near the beginning of the report.
Of the following, the MOST important reason for doing this is that it
    A. facilitates organizing the material clearly
    B. assures that all the topics will be covered
    C. avoids unnecessary repetition of ideas
    D. prepares the reader for the facts that will follow

    4.____

5. You have been asked to write a report on methods of hiring and training new employees. Your report is going to be about ten pages long.
   For the convenience of your readers, a brief summary of your findings should
   A. appear at the beginning of your report
   B. be appended to the report as a postscript
   C. be circulated in a separate memo
   D. be inserted in tabular form in the middle of your report

6. In preparing a report, the MAIN reason for writing an outline is usually to
   A. help organize thoughts in a logical sequence
   B. provide a guide for the typing of the report
   C. allow the ultimate user to review the report in advance
   D. ensure that the report is being prepared on schedule

7. The one of the following which is MOST appropriate as a reason for including footnotes in a report is to
   A. correct capitalization
   B. delete passages
   C. improve punctuation
   D. cite references

8. A completed formal report may contain all of the following EXCEPT
   A. a synopsis
   B. a preface
   C. marginal notes
   D. bibliographical references

9. Of the following, the MAIN use of proofreaders' marks is to
   A. explain corrections to be made
   B. indicate that a manuscript has been read and approved
   C. let the reader know who proofread the report
   D. indicate the format of the report

10. Informative, readable, and concise reports have been found to observe the following rules:
    Rule I. Keep the report short and easy to understand
    Rule II. Vary the length of sentences.
    Rule III. Vary the style of sentences so that, for example, they are not all just subject-verb, subject-verb.
    Consider this hospital laboratory report: The experiment was started in January. The apparatus was put together in six weeks. At that time, the synthesizing process was begun. The synthetic chemicals were separated. Then they were used in tests on patients.
    Which one of the following choices MOST accurately classifies the above rules into those which are violated by this report ad those which are not?
    A. II is violated, but I and III are not.
    B. III is violated, but I and II are not.
    C. II and III are violated, but I is not.
    D. I, II, and III are violated,

Questions 11-13.

DIRECTIONS: Questions 11 through 13 are based on the following example of a report. The report consists of eight numbered sentences, some of which are not consistent with the principles of good report writing.

(1) I interviewed Mrs. Loretta Crawford in Room 424 of County Hospital. (2) She had collapsed on the street and been brought into emergency. (3) She is an attractive woman with many friends judging by the cards she had received. (4) She did not know what her husband's last job had been, or what their present income was. (5) The first thing that Mrs. Crawford said was that she had never worked and that her husband was presently unemployed. (6) She did not know if they had any medical coverage or if they could pay the bill. (7) She said that her husband could not be reached by telephone but that he would be in to see her that afternoon. (8) I left word at the nursing station to be called when he arrived.

11. A good report should be arranged in logical order.
    Which of the following sentences from the report does NOT appear in its proper sequence in the report?
    A. 1 B. 4 C. 7 D. 8

12. Only material that is relevant to the main thought of a report should be included.
    Which of the following sentences from the report contains material which is LEAST relevant to this report? Sentence
    A. 3 B. 4 C. 6 D. 8

13. Reports should include all essential information.
    Of the following, the MOST important fact that is missing from this report is:
    A. Who was involved in the interview
    B. What was discovered at the interview
    C. When the interview took place
    D. Where the interview took place

Questions 14-15.

DIRECTIONS: Each of Questions 14 and 15 consists of four numbered sentences which constitute a paragraph in a report. They are not in the right order. Choose the numbered arrangement appearing after letter A, B, C, or D which is MOST logical and which BEST expresses the thought of the paragraph.

14. I. Congress made the commitment explicit in the Housing Act of 1949, establishing as a national goal the realization of a decent home and suitable environment for every American family.
    II. The result has been that the goal of decent home and suitable environment is still as far distant as ever for the disadvantaged urban family
    III. In spite of this action by Congress, federal housing programs have continued to be fragmented and grossly under-funded.
    IV. The passage of the National Housing Act signaled a new federal commitment to provide housing for the nation's citizens.

4 (#2)

The CORRECT answer is:
A. I, IV, III, II   B. IV, I, III, II   C. IV, I, III, II   D. II, IV, I, III

15.
   I. The greater expense does not necessarily involve "exploitation," but it is often perceived as exploitative and unfair by those who are aware of the price differences involved, but unaware of operating costs.
   II. Ghetto residents believe they are "exploited" by local merchants, and evidence substantiates some of these beliefs.
   III. However, stores in low-income areas were more likely to be small independents, which could not achieve the economies available to supermarket chains and were, therefore, more likely to charge higher prices, and the customers were more likely to buy smaller-sized packages which are more expensive per unit of measure.
   IV. A study conducted in one city showed that distinctly higher prices were charged for goods sold in ghetto stores than in other areas.

   The CORRECT answer is:
   A. IV, II, I, III   B. IV, I, III, II   C. II, IV, III, I   D. II, III, IV, I

15.____

16. In organizing data to be presented in a formal report, the FIRST of the following steps should be
    A. determining the conclusions to be drawn
    B. establishing the time sequence of the data
    C. sorting and arranging like data into groups
    D. evaluating how consistently the data support the recommendations

16.____

17. All reports should be prepared with at least one copy so that
    A. there is one copy for your file
    B. there is a copy for your supervisor
    C. the report can be sent to more than one person
    D. the person getting the report can forward a copy to someone else

17.____

18. Before turning in a report of an investigation he has made, a supervisor discovers some additional information he did not include in this report. Whether he rewrites this report to include this additional information should PRIMARILY depend on the
    A. importance of the report itself
    B. number of people who will eventually review this report
    C. established policy covering the subject matter of the report
    D. bearing this new information has on the conclusions of the report

18.____

KEY (CORRECT ANSWERS)

1.	A	11.	B
2.	A	12.	A
3.	D	13.	C
4.	D	14.	B
5.	A	15.	C
6.	A	16.	C
7.	D	17.	A
8.	C	18.	D
9.	A		
10.	C		

www.ingramcontent.com/pod-product-compliance
Lightning Source LLC
Chambersburg PA
CBHW081829300426
44116CB00014B/2523